The Baldrige Workbook for Healthcare

Donald C. Fisher, Ph.D.
Bryan P. Simmons, M.D.

QUALITY RESOURCES®
A Division of The Kraus Organization Limited
New York, New York

Most Quality Resources books are available at quantity discounts when purchased in bulk. For more information contact:

Special Sales Department
Quality Resources
A Division of The Kraus Organization Limited
902 Broadway
New York, New York 10010
800-247-8519

Copyright © 1996   Donald C. Fisher, Ph.D. and
                   Bryan P. Simmons, M.D.

All rights reserved. No part of this work covered by the copyrights hereon may be reproduced or used in any form or by any means--graphic, electronic, or mechanical, including photocopying, recording, taping, or information storage and retrieval systems--without written permission of the publisher.

Printed in the United States of America

00 99 98 97 96   10 9 8 7 6 5 4 3 2 1

Quality Resources
A Division of The Kraus Organization Limited
902 Broadway
New York, New York 10010
212-979-8600
800-247-8519

The paper used in this publication meets the minimum requirements of American National Standard for Information Sciences--Permanence of Paper for Printed Library Materials, ANSI Z39.48-1984.

ISBN 0-527-76313-6

To my children

Candice, Chase, and Channing Fisher

Three quality miracles in progress.

DCF

To my father

Carl Simmons

Who taught me to pursue excellence
and quality in all my endeavors.

BPS

CONTENTS

Foreword vii

Preface ix

Part I — The Baldrige Joint Commission Accreditation Standards

Introduction xi

Chapter One: How to Use this Workbook 1

Chapter Two: Assessment Scoring System 11

Part II — The Baldrige Categories Incorporating Joint Commission Standards

Chapter Three: Leadership 25

Chapter Four: Information and Analysis 47

Chapter Five: Strategic Planning 67

Chapter Six: Human Resource Development and Management 83

Chapter Seven: Process Management 111

Chapter Eight: Organizational Performance Results 157

Chapter Nine: Focus on and Satisfaction of Patients
               and Other Stakeholders 181

Part III — The Strategic Plan for the Health Care Organization

Chapter Ten: Transforming Assessment Findings into Actionable Strategies for Improvement 227

Glossary 237

Appendix A: Malcolm Baldrige National Quality Award for Health Care Organizations Written Application Checklist 245

Appendix B: Health Care Organizational Assessment 249

Appendix C: Benchmarking Process Checklist 261

Appendix D: Reference List for Additional Reading 267

Appendix E: Interviewing Hints and Tips 269

Appendix F: How to Order Copies of the Health Care Pilot Criteria 271

FOREWORD

On August 20, 1987, President Ronald Reagan signed the Malcolm Baldrige Quality Improvement Act into law. The purpose of the legislation was to promote quality awareness and practices in U.S. business, recognize quality achievements of U.S. companies and publicize successful quality strategies and programs. The core of the legislation was the creation of the Malcolm Baldrige National Quality Award. The Baldrige Award Criteria, developed by quality experts and refined each year, detail the requirements for achieving world-class quality.

The Baldrige Criteria provide a common language and framework for organizations that seek to improve operational and financial performance and enhance customer satisfaction. One of the most beneficial aspects of the award process is that the Criteria provide a proven diagnostic system to assess organizational design, process, and performance. While many companies are aware of their shortcomings before the application process, the review of external experts adds validity to an internal assessment of progress. Over 400 hours of rigorous review by quality experts are given to applicants who pass the four stages of review. The feedback report provided to each applicant is invaluable. The report specifically identifies strengths and areas for improvement. The report can serve as the foundation and framework for an organization's strategic planning process.

The growth of interest in the award has been phenomenal. Today, two-thirds of the states have Baldrige-based award programs. A myriad of local awards have been developed. Many countries have developed Baldrige-based awards to stimulate a focus on quality and improvement. Major companies have also used the criteria to develop a president's or chairman's award to stimulate internal emphasis on improvement. The Baldrige staff report that over 1 million copies of the Criteria have been distributed.

The Baldrige process has also provided new avenues for the transfer of information. The annual Quest for Excellence Conference features Baldrige winners. These companies proudly share their successful strategies and techniques with others. Through highlighting concepts such as benchmarking, organizations seeking to improve processes can find partners willing to engage in benchmarking efforts. The twenty-four companies selected as winners of the prestigious award are serving as role models for industries in the U.S. and across the world.

The Malcolm Baldrige Award began a new era in 1995 when the two-year Health Care Pilot was implemented. Since 1993, a group of concerned health care professionals have worked with the Baldrige staff to develop a set of criteria that would encourage excellence in the U.S. health care industry. The goals of the Health Care Pilot are to determine the sector's readiness for an award process and the capability of health care organizations, to test eligibility rules, and to determine the response to a Baldrige-based award.

The Baldrige Criteria, while similar to existing criteria, are tailored to the specifics of the health care industry. The Criteria are designed to help health care organizations improve by meeting dual, results-oriented goals: 1) delivery of ever-improving value to patients and other stakeholders, contributing to improved health care quality, and 2) improvement of overall organizational effectiveness, use of resources, and capabilities.

The response to the pilot was very positive; 44 health care organizations applied. This year at the Quest for Excellence conference several of these organizations will present their stories of success and the work remaining to be accomplished.

As the pilot enters its second year, there are many unanswered questions about the program and its future. Can the Baldrige Criteria enhance organizational and financial performance in health care organizations? Will the Criteria provide the same framework for excellence that the private business sector has experienced? Will health care organizations be willing to benchmark and share data? Can we learn how to standardize health care processes and reduce variation in clinical care?

Health care organizations are concerned about the quality of care and the new demands of patients and payers. Many are taking steps to enhance customer satisfaction and organizational performance using the Baldrige framework. For example, many health care organizations have already applied for and some have been recognized as winners in state Baldrige-based award programs.

This book will help you understand the nuances of the Health Care Criteria and its value to improving your organizational performance and customer satisfaction. The tools included will help you guide your quality journey and inspire you to achieve new levels of productivity, employee involvement, customer satisfaction, and loyalty. You provide the passion and direction and let the Criteria provide the roadmap.

— Ellen Gaucher
Senior Associate Director
University of Michigan Hospital

PREFACE

Many health care organizations are beginning to embrace the concepts of total quality management. Some are doing so to comply with the new direction of the Joint Commission on Accreditation of Health Care Organizations (JCAHO), which has encouraged health care organizations to seek continuous improvement. Other organizations want to pursue world-class practices and thus are considering applying for the new Malcolm Baldrige Award for Health Care. We designed this book to be useful for those who want to either apply for the Baldrige Award or use the Baldrige Criteria to assess their performance, as a stepping-stone toward improvement.

Because most health care organizations seek accreditation from JCAHO, we also included references to the JCAHO standards. This book is not intended to replace the JCAHO accreditation manual. However, it is a tool to evaluate a health care organization using the Baldrige Criteria without losing sight of JCAHO's important role in health care accreditation.

We would like to thank Cinda Kinsey and Cynthia Caudle with Methodist Health Systems in Memphis, Tennessee for their thorough review of this book and their comments. Both professionals understand and have extensive experience using the Malcolm Baldrige National Quality Award Criteria and the Joint Commission on Accreditation of Health Care Organizations (JCAHO) compliance standards and how both standards apply to health care organizations.

Part I The Baldrige Joint Commission Accreditation Standards

INTRODUCTION

The quality improvement movement is sweeping the health care industry just as it is sweeping other industries in the United States. All parties interested in health care are demanding more value for their health care dollars. Hospitals and other health care organizations have attempted to cut costs while preserving quality. Many have responded by beginning programs for total quality management; such programs are often called continuous quality improvement (CQI) when applied to health care.

Baldrige Award Promotes a Model for Excellence

The Malcolm Baldrige National Quality Award was started in 1987 to stimulate improved competitiveness in U. S. business. Awards were to be given in three categories—manufacturing, service, and small business—with no more than two awards per category per year. Not-for-profit health care institutions were not eligible to receive the award. However, a Baldrige award that is specific to health care was piloted in 1995. The assessment process for the award provides health care organizations with a comprehensive framework for evaluating their quality processes. Because both Baldrige and the Joint Commission on Accreditation of Health Care Organizations (JCAHO) base their evaluation on CQI, there are many similarities between the two evaluations (see Table 1). The Baldrige Criteria are specifically linked to an award for excellence. However, many institutions use the Baldrige Criteria as an assessment tool rather than a way to win recognition. Institutions that score high on a Baldrige assessment in any area are believed to have world-class practices in that area.

A Separate Baldrige Award for Health Care Organizations

Some Baldrige examiners believe there should not be a specific Baldrige award for health care. However, there are at least two important differences among health care and other industrial settings that create the need for a separate award: 1) two management structures, and 2) problems making valid benchmarking comparisons between hospitals. The industrial model of CQI assumes one management structure. In the hospital there are two management structures, the hospital administration and the medical staff. Usually the medical staff makes very important decisions about patient care with little or no input from administration. This is particularly true for physicians in private practice. In health maintenance organizations (HMOs) physicians are usually employees of the organization. Regardless of the employee status of the physician, patients with similar illnesses often receive different treatments. Clinical practice guidelines and critical pathways are sometimes used to standardize treatments and reduce variation in practices. However, even with such standardized treatment outlines, patient care can never be as uniform as a manufacturing process. Physicians will continue to use their professional judgment to deviate from patient care outlines.

The second reason for a separate Baldrige award for health care organizations is the problem with comparing and benchmarking patient outcome data. The outcomes of care are the most direct evidence of its efficacy, and so variations in outcomes are being used increasingly to compare systems of care. Changes in outcomes should be used cautiously because they may represent changes in the system itself or changes in inputs into the system. In an industrial setting, variations in inputs are an acknowledged problem area for quality management, and many plans for improving industrial quality begin with assuring the quality of raw materials. In health care settings, many processes are determined by the needs of the patient, and many outcomes, such as mortality, are strongly determined by patient characteristics. Thus, for both process and outcome, patient characteristics can play a more important role than does organizational policy in determining how much variation is measured. In order to validly compare health care systems on the basis of outcomes, sources of variation that are not controllable by the system need to be taken into account. There have been a number of attempts to do this by the use of severity-of-illness adjustments or stratifying data; that is, comparing apples to apples. JCAHO hopes to provide valid benchmarking data for both outcomes and processes through IMSystem, but their approach remains controversial.

JCAHO Promotes Continuous Quality Improvement

JCAHO began to promote CQI in 1986 with its "Agenda for Change." The specific objectives of this agenda were the following: 1) revision and reorganization of Joint Commission standards, first to reduce their number and complexity and refocus them on clinical, support, management, and governance functions that are most important to patient health outcomes, and second, to foster continuous improvement in performance of these functions and in their outcomes; 2) improvement in the survey process to direct greater attention to the effectiveness of collaboration and integration throughout the entire organization in performing these functions and in continuously improving them; and 3) establishment of a national performance measurement system, called IMSystem, that includes uniform, objective measures of each organization's performance and a resultant reference database that permits comparison with the performance of other organizations. Before the Agenda for Change, JCAHO focused on an organization's capability to provide quality care but did little to assess actual performance. Now, JCAHO will focus on whether quality care was actually delivered.

Health Care Organizations Seek JCAHO Accreditation

Most health care organizations seek JCAHO accreditation to satisfy laws that require such organizations to meet certain standards before they can fully function. A JCAHO accreditation application is not an application for excellence, nor does JCAHO accreditation imply world-class practices. Instead, JCAHO accreditation is intended to show that the health care organization is in overall compliance with acceptable standards of care. Until IMSystem is in place, it is not even clear that an organization can use JCAHO accreditation to benchmark its practices against the best in the country. However, JCAHO does offer "accreditation with commendation" for organizations with a score of 90 or higher for all applicable services. The other accreditation results include "accreditation", "provisional accreditation" (for those organizations not yet ready for a full evaluation), and "not accredited".

The key elements of CQI are embedded in the JCAHO accreditation requirements. Thus, an institution can use the accreditation manual and "Score 100", the JCAHO's computer-based survey preparation tool, to prepare the entire organization for CQI. However, JCAHO has stopped short of requiring CQI or any other method of improvement. Methods are less important than results.

Physician Participation in Quality

Health care institutions across the country are trying a variety of methods to increase the participation of physicians in quality management practices, including clinical practice guidelines. Most of these efforts are a long way from fully integrating physicians in CQI. Until this integration is more substantial, it seems unlikely that any organization will receive the Baldrige Award. Many physicians believe that the road to quality should be one of personal improvement for all health care workers. Although no one can deny that personal improvements and expertise contribute greatly to quality efforts, most quality managers believe that systems improvements and teamwork play the dominant role in quality management. Physicians often overlook the importance of teamwork to providing error-free, quality medicine. Physicians are trained to believe that an error is a failure of character—someone wasn't careful enough or didn't try hard enough. Thus, errors and other efforts of poor quality are often perceived by physicians as being someone's fault. Fault-finding forms the basis of peer review, a quality improvement system used frequently by medical staff members. Physicians have been willing to invest many hours in peer review, and thus, time constraints aren't the only important deterrent to physician participation in CQI. It doesn't seem likely that physicians will participate fully in CQI until they change the way they think about how quality can best be improved.

Baldrige and Joint Commission Criteria Used to Evaluate Organizations

Both the JCAHO accreditation process and the new Baldrige assessment for health care can be used to evaluate the current status of an organization's quality processes. Both should provide good information about the strengths and weaknesses of such processes. However, too much emphasis on Baldrige may cause an organization to overlook basic processes needed for accreditation, even though these processes are not critical to ensuring quality. Receiving JCAHO accreditation also may not be enough of a stimulus for an organization to sharpen its competitive edge to survive in the tumultuous years ahead. Thus, both processes are worthy of consideration by organizations which want to prosper. For these organizations we hope to explain how JCAHO and the Baldrige Criteria are interrelated.

	JCAHO	Baldrige (Health Care Pilot Criteria)
Founded	1951	1995
Purpose	Ensures compliance with acceptable standards of care.	Promote, recognize, and publicize quality U.S. health care organizations. Increase competitiveness and productivity.
Quality Philosophy	Continuous Quality Improvement (CQI) or Total Quality Management (TQM).	Continuous Quality Improvement.
Eligibility	Hospitals; centers for substance abuse and the mentally retarded; long-term care, home care, ambulatory care, laboratory services, and networks.	All health care organizations.
Value to Organization	Allows medicare participation; ensures compliance with standards; gives a framework for CQI; benchmarking when IMSystem is fully established.	Self-assessment; benchmarking; recognition.
Timing of Evaluations	Every three years.	Must reapply each time.
Confidentiality	Much data open to public release.	Data confidential.

TABLE 1

Comparing Joint Commission to Baldrige

Both the Joint commission on Accreditation of Healthcare Organizations (JCAHO) and the Baldrige Criteria base their evaluations of health care institutions on the principles of continuous quality improvement (CQI). Thus, there are many similarities between the two evaluations, but there are also many differences. The JCAHO standards are outlined in the *Comprehensive Accreditation Manual for Hospitals*[1] (see pp. 242 and 271). These standards are divided into three sections: Patients Rights and Organizational Ethics, Organizational Functions, and Structures with Functions.

The first two sections of JCAHO are subdivided into important functions. There are currently eleven different important functions (soon to be 15). These functions are the following: 1) patient rights and organizational ethics, 2) assessment of patients, 3) care of patients, 4) education, 5) continuum of care, 6) improving organizational performance, 7) leadership, 8) management of environment of care, 9) management of human resources, 10) management of information, and 11) surveillance, prevention, and control of infection.

Each of these important functions has nine dimensions of performance: efficacy, appropriateness, availability, timeliness, effectiveness, continuity, safety, efficiency, and respect and caring. The last of the three main sections, Structures with Functions, is subdivided into chapters on governance, management, medical staff, and nursing.

Baldrige Criteria versus Joint Commission Compliance Standards

The Baldrige assessment framework is quite different from JCAHO's framework. Criteria, core values, and concepts are organized into the following seven categories: leadership, information and analysis, strategic planning, human resource development and management, process management, organizational performance results, and focus on satisfaction of patients and other stakeholders. The different framework of Baldrige and JCAHO criteria make direct comparison of their standards difficult. Most Baldrige Criteria do not have a single JCAHO standard that is analogous. Thus, there is no easy crosswalk between the two sets of standards.

Comparing scoring between Baldrige and JCAHO criteria is also difficult. Baldrige scores are determined by comparing ideal to actual performance in each of the seven categories. JCAHO scores are much more difficult to compute, and one needs to refer to the accreditation manual, including the chapter "The Accreditation Decision Process" and individual scoring guidelines, because JCAHO scores are derived from specific scoring guidelines rather than the more general standards. Some JCAHO scores are "capped" at high values to prevent low scores that result from new standards that are

---

[1] Available from the Joint Commission on Accreditation of Healthcare Organizations, One Renaissance Boulevard, Oakbrook Terrace, IL 60181-9887.

not yet fully implemented. Thus, one cannot easily compute JCAHO scores that compare directly with Baldrige scores.

Another difference between Baldrige and JCAHO scoring is that JCAHO scoring guidelines are often very specific and the Baldrige Criteria are more general. For example, JCAHO scoring guidelines require blood and surgical case review. The Baldrige Criteria are not nearly this specific but mention efforts to ensure quality, effectiveness, and efficiency of services, which presumably include blood and surgical case review. Each general Baldrige standard may encompass a large number of specific JCAHO requirements that are listed in the scoring guidelines. In summary, Baldrige and JCAHO standards are both based on the concepts of CQI but differ in so many respects that direct comparison is difficult. Each set of standards can be useful to an organization and should be seen as complementing one another rather than being directly comparable.

Baldrige Criteria for Health Care Organizations as an Assessment Tool

The Baldrige Award Criteria for Health Care were first piloted in 1995 and received enormous interest from health care professionals throughout the world. The Baldrige Criteria for Health Care, as well as its counterpart criteria, have been criticized as being too cumbersome and too complicated to be understood and easily used for organizational assessments.

In contrast, this workbook presents the Baldrige Criteria for Health Care in a simplified format that allows a cross-functional team of health care professionals to conduct a self-assessment of their organization. To enhance the value of the assessment process for the health care organizaton, zero-based and world-class examples are provided. In addition, examples of related JCAHO compliance issues are aligned with the Baldrige Criteria throughout the workbook to provide further examples for the team to consider while conducting their organizational assessment.

CHAPTER ONE

How to Use this Workbook

How to Use this Workbook

This workbook is designed to serve as an easy-to-use guide for employee teams within health care organizations to assess and score their organization's quality efforts using the Malcolm Baldrige National Quality Award Criteria for Health Care. It also allows them to check their organization's Joint Commission compliance as it relates to the Baldrige Criteria.

This workbook can be used to provide a quality check for an organization's continuous improvement efforts, to help employees understand what the Baldrige Criteria for Health Care are asking, to gauge their organization's compliance against Joint Commission standards, and to provide a template for an organization's self-assessment and strategic planning efforts. In addition, this workbook provides guidance for employees and employee teams to score their departments or total organization in 62 areas. It also serves as an annual benchmark for improvement and offers a strategic planning guide for short-term and longer-term planning. This workbook assists employees in determining their organization's readiness to apply for various state, national, and professional association quality awards that are based on the Baldrige Criteria. This workbook can be used to help employees collect organizational data to write their quality award application.

How to Begin and Prepare for an Assessment

The assessment of an organization should begin with the full support and sponsorship of the senior executives and health care staff leaders. The senior leadership should appoint an assessment team administrator.

The first step in preparing for the assessment should include conducting a Baldrige assessment briefing for senior leadership. This session can be conducted by the organization's training director or the person who has been selected by senior leaders as the assessment team administrator to oversee the assessment process. The person(s) responsible for the briefing should review this workbook and have a thorough understanding of total quality management, the Baldrige Criteria as it relates to health care organizations, and Joint Commission standards before conducting the session.

In addition, senior executives and health care staff leadership must be educated in the principles of Total Quality Management (TQM) in order for them to appreciate the value of conducting an organizational assessment. Several activities are recommended to help senior leaders develop an understanding of quality principles. These include the following:

- Reading quality books and articles (suggested resource list included in Appendix D of this workbook).
- Reviewing the Malcolm Baldrige National Quality Award Criteria for Health Care (included throughout this workbook).
- Benchmarking other health care organizations to review best practices (see Appendix C).

After the senior executives and health care staff leadership have been briefed, they should begin the process of soliciting assessment team members. Many organizations solicit members through in-house employee newsletters, electronic mail, or personal letters sent from the CEO or president inviting participation. Team member selections should be considered from staff who have expressed an interest in better understanding and using the Baldrige Criteria for Health Care and Joint Commission standards as a template for improving their organization.

Once team members have been selected, plan a two-day assessment workshop that can be conducted by staff members who have an understanding of the Baldrige Criteria for Health Care and Joint Commission standards. The workshop may include using a case study (available from National Institute of Standards and Technology, Rt. 70 and Quince Orchard Rd., Administration Building, Room A537, Gaithersburg, MD 20899-0001) for the team to practice identifying organizational strengths and opportunities for improvement. During the workshop the team will discuss each category and determine "What does it mean for my organization?" The use of this workbook will help the team practice translating the Baldrige Criteria for Health Care and Joint Commission compliance issues into simple language for their own organizationwide assessment.

ASSESSING THE INSTITUTION

Team Member Selection

Assessment team members should represent a cross section of staff in the selection process. All disciplines, departments, and professional levels throughout the organization should be represented on the teams. Diversity adds value and strength to each assessment team.

Team Leader Selection

In larger organizations, seven Baldrige category subteams can be developed. A Subject Matter Expert (SME) for a particular Baldrige category can be selected as the category team leader. In smaller organizations where there are a limited number of personnel who can serve on assessment teams, all seven Baldrige categories can be assessed by one team.

How to Use this Workbook   3

ASSESSMENT TEAM COMPOSITION (LARGE ORGANIZATION)
(20 to 40 Members)

Team 1
Leadership

- Senior Administrator (Team Leader)
- Director of Nursing
- Physician
- Nurse
- Manager
- Pharmacist

Team 2
Information & Analysis

- VP - Information Systems (Team Leader)
- Nurse
- Department Head
- Manager
- Physician
- Pharmacist

Team 3
Strategic Planning

- Assistant Administrator (Team Leader)
- Manager
- Department Head
- Dietitian
- Medical Records Staff
- Director of Safety

Team 4
Human Resource Development and Management

- VP - Human Resources (Team Leader)
- Nurse
- Department Head
- Manager
- Admissions Staff
- Housekeeping Staff

Team 5
Process Management

- VP - Operations (Team Leader)
- Nurse
- Department Head
- Manager
- Medical Staff
- Admissions Staff

Team 6
Organizational Performance Results

- VP - Finance (Team Leader)
- Physician
- Department Head
- Manager
- Medical Staff
- Admissions Staff

Team 7
Focus on and Satisfaction of Patients and Other Stakeholders

- VP - Marketing (Team Leader)
- Dietitian
- Nurse
- Department Head
- Medical Staff
- Admissions Staff
- Housekeeping Staff

ASSESSMENT TEAM COMPOSITION (SMALL ORGANIZATION)
(6 to 8 members)

Team Assesses All Seven Baldrige Categories

- Senior Administrator (Team Leader)
- Physician
- Nurse
- Manager
- Department Head
- Dietitian
- Pharmacist
- Physical Rehabilitation Therapist

Pre-assessment Meeting for Each Baldrige Category Team

Each Baldrige category team should hold a pre-assessment planning meeting to identify individuals to be interviewed during the assessment. Dates and interview times need to be agreed upon during this session and an agenda and timetable should be prepared. After the team selects the individuals to be interviewed, a team member needs to contact all persons to be interviewed.

Coordination of Assessment Team Schedules

The assessment team administrator should coordinate all seven category team schedules with team leaders and develop an overall assessment plan and timetable. This schedule and timetable should then be submitted to senior executive and health care staff leadership for review and approval.

Team Interviews of Selected Participants

After approval has been secured from senior leadership, each team is ready to begin its interview process with its selected participants. The entire Baldrige category team will take turns interviewing the participants. This allows for more interaction and input for the assessment team. During the interview process all assessment team members will have a copy of this workbook in hand and will make notes under each of the questions. Each category team may choose to interview two or three groups of participants representing various levels throughout the organization. Interview hints and tips are provided in Appendix E.

Assessment Team Consensus and Scoring of the Category

After all category interviews have been completed the category team leaders will hold a consensus review meeting. All team members will review the areas identified as strengths and opportunities for improvement in both Baldrige for health care organizations and Joint Commission compliance issues. The team will reach a consensus and assign each item a percentile score and will ultimately award the category a total point score. All scores will be based on the Baldrige scoring process.

Entire Assessment Report Consolidated and Delivered

All seven Baldrige category teams will deliver their assessment findings to the assessment team administrator. The assessment team administrator will meet with all category team leaders to review results and findings regarding the organization's compliance against the Baldrige Criteria. Joint Commission issues related to the seven categories are noted for each item.

After the assessment team administrator and all seven category team leaders have reached a consensus on the strengths, opportunities for improvement, category percentile scores, and

How to Use this Workbook 5

the overall assessment point score, the assessment is finalized. The completed assessment is then delivered to senior executive and health care staff leadership. The entire assessment process usually takes from one to two months to complete.

SEVEN STEPS FOR SUCCESSFUL ASSESSMENT IMPLEMENTATION AND WORKBOOK USE

The following seven steps will further explain how this workbook will be useful in simplifying the assessment process for the health care organization.

STEP ONE — READ BALDRIGE CRITERIA

After the team or teams have been formed, members should read the Baldrige Award Criteria for Health Care that appear at the beginning of each item throughout this workbook. Under each item summary the Baldrige Criteria for Health Care appear under the heading "Areas to Address."

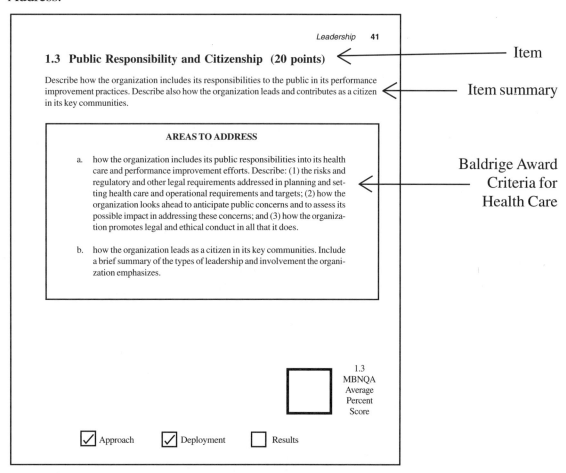

The Baldrige Criteria notes that are used to better explain the intent of the Criteria have been eliminated and incorporated into the simplified questions that appear throughout this workbook.

6 THE BALDRIGE WORKBOOK FOR HEALTHCARE

STEP TWO | REVIEW QUESTIONS

Following the Areas to Address pages of this workbook are questions based on the Baldrige Criteria for Health Care. This workbook takes all the Baldrige Criteria and breaks them down into simple questions so they are more understandable and user-friendly. This allows a clearer and more precise organizational assessment to be conducted.

The questions are to be asked of different levels of staff throughout the organization. The assessment team should divide this task among its members.

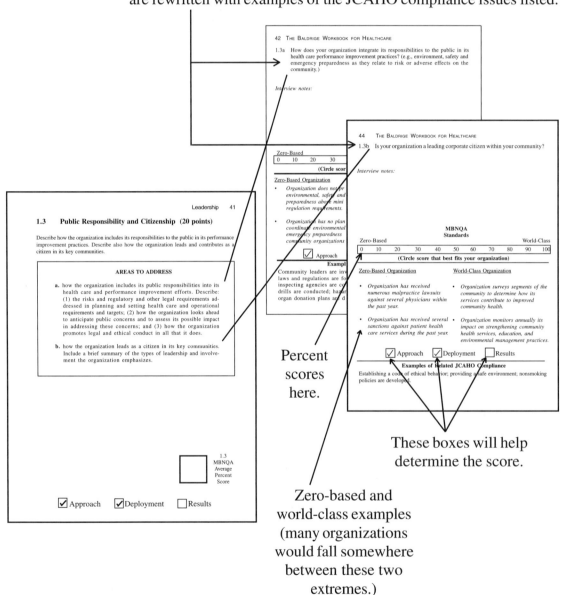

Simplified questions based on the Baldrige Criteria for Health Care are rewritten with examples of the JCAHO compliance issues listed.

Percent scores here.

These boxes will help determine the score.

Zero-based and world-class examples (many organizations would fall somewhere between these two extremes.)

How to Use this Workbook   7

STEP THREE — REVIEW ZERO-BASED AND WORLD-CLASS EXAMPLES

Before recording answers to the questions, review the examples of zero-based organizations and world-class organizations that appear on the bottom third of the page.

Below the examples at the bottom of the page appear three boxes labelled *Approach, Deployment,* and *Results.* These boxes will aid in assessing the kinds of information and/or data the question requires. (Refer to Assessment Scoring System—Chapter 2.)

STEP FOUR — MAKE NOTES DURING THE INTERVIEW

In the middle of the page under each question is an *interview notes* section for recording answers to the questions given by staff members as they are being interviewed by the assessment team. This data should be collected and reviewed before listing strengths and opportunities for improvement on the opposite page.

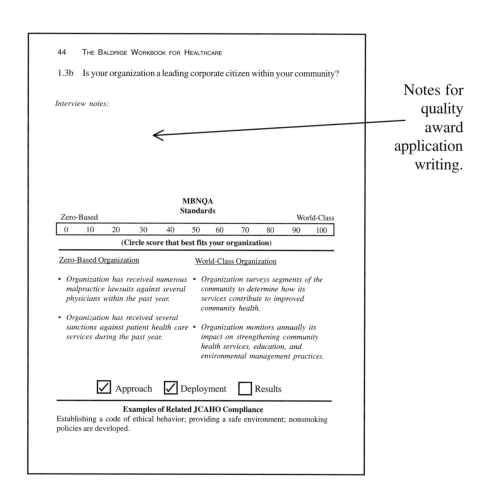

Notes for quality award application writing.

8 THE BALDRIGE WORKBOOK FOR HEALTHCARE

| STEP FIVE | LIST COMMENTS FOR STRENGTHS AND IMPROVEMENT

On the opposing page the question is restated. After the interviews are completed, review the interview notes. The team will then list the organization's strengths and opportunities for improvement. All comments should be written in short, complete sentence form.

Comments should be written in complete sentences.

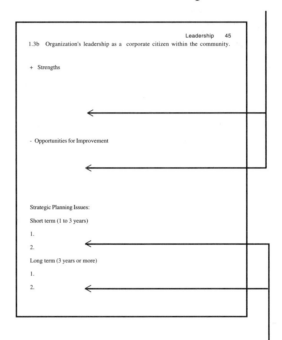

List short-term and long-term strategic planning issues.

| STEP SIX | LIST STRATEGIC PLANNING ISSUES

After reviewing the interview notes and listing strengths and opportunities for improvement related to Baldrige Criteria requirements and Joint Commission compliance issues, the assessment team should select and list any short-term and long-term strategic planning issues. This data can be used later when developing a strategic plan for the organization.

| STEP SEVEN | SCORE ASSESSMENT ITEMS

The assessment is broken down into seven Baldrige categories:

 1.0 Leadership
 2.0 Information and Analysis

How to Use this Workbook   9

3.0 Strategic Planning
4.0 Human Resource Development and Management
5.0 Process Management
6.0 Organizational Performance Results
7.0 Focus on and Satisfaction of Patients and Other Stakeholders

These seven categories are divided into Baldrige assessment items (i.e., 1.1, 1.2, 1.3, 2.1, 2.2...) and the 28 assessment items are broken down into areas (i.e., 1.1a, 1.1b,...). The percent score is reflective of the strengths and opportunities for improvement of the areas within each assessment item. Thus, throughout the assessment all items will obtain a percent score based on the Baldrige scoring system. In addition, within all areas of the assessment process JCAHO compliance issues appear. All assessment item percent scores will be transferred to the Summary of Assessment Items score sheet located at the end of chapter 9.

The assessment scores will ultimately be reviewed, prioritized, and transformed into actionable strategies for improvement. The transformation process is explained in detail in chapter 10 of this workbook.

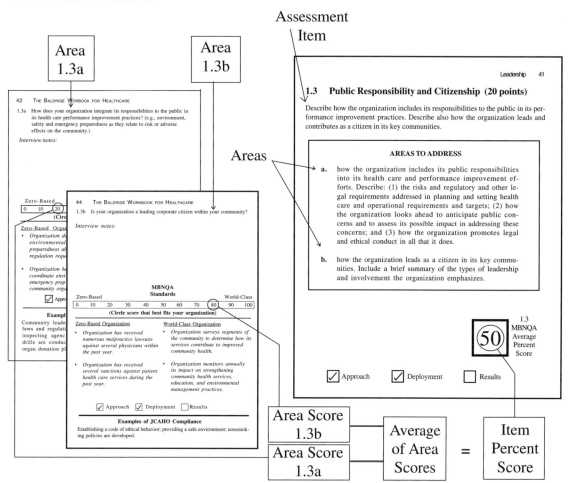

CHAPTER TWO

Assessment Scoring System

The Baldrige scoring system is based on three evaluation dimensions: (1) Approach, (2) Deployment, and (3) Results. All three dimensions should be considered before assigning a percentage score. In addition, each of the categories assessed will have Scoring Profiles to help facilitate the scoring process.

Approach

Approach refers to the methods the organization uses to achieve purposes addressed in the assessment categories. The scoring criteria used to evaluate approaches include one or more of the following, as appropriate:

- The appropriateness of the methods, tools, and techniques to the requirements.
- The effectiveness of the use of methods, tools, and techniques.
- The degree to which the approach is systematic, integrated, and consistently applied.
- The degree to which the approach embodies effective evaluation/improvement cycles.
- The degree to which the approach is based upon quantitative information that is objective and reliable.
- The degree to which the approach is prevention-based.
- The indicators of unique and innovative approaches, including significant and effective new adaptations of tools and techniques used in other applications or types of organizations.

Deployment

Deployment refers to the extent to which the approaches are applied to all relevant areas and activities addressed and implied in the assessment categories. The scoring criteria used to evaluate deployment include one or more of the following, as appropriate:

- The appropriateness and effective application by all work units to all processes and activities.
- The appropriate and effective application to all program and service features.
- The appropriate and effective application to all transactions and interactions with faculty, staff, students, stakeholders, suppliers, and the public.

Results

Results refers to outcomes and effects in achieving the purposes addressed and implied in the assessment categories. The scoring criteria used to evaluate results include one or more of the following:

- The quality and performance levels demonstrated and their importance.
- The rate of quality and performance improvement.
- The breadth of quality and performance improvement.
- The demonstration of sustained improvement.
- The comparison with competitive organizations and other leading educational providers.
- The organization's ability to show the improvements derive from its quality practices and actions.

The percent scores range from a low of 0% for a zero-based organization to a high of 100% for a world-class organization. An organization can be 0% in some areas and 100% (world class) in others. The anchor point is 50% which is middle range. Many organizations fall below the 50% anchor point. The 50% anchor point is considered to be good, but certainly below what an organization that is striving to be the "best-in-class" among leading organizations would score.

Zero-Based					50% Anchor Point					World-Class	
0	10	20	30	40	50	60	70	80	90	100

(Organizations that score 0% have an anecdotal approach, lack deployment, and have no meaningful results.)

(Organizations that score 100% reflect a refined, very mature approach, deployed and well-adapted in all relevant areas.)

Approach and Deployment

Approach and deployment are considered together. This is because without deployment, an approach would merely represent an idea or a plan. The Baldrige Criteria are based heavily upon "successful quality strategies" that advocate approaches that are implemented and deployed.

SCORING GUIDELINES

		Approach/Deployment	Results
World Class	100%	• A very strong, fact-based improvement process approach is fully deployed.	• Current performance is excellent in most areas. • Strong evidence of industry and benchmark leadership.
	80%	• A sound, systematic approach and deployment in most areas of organization, and strong integration with the strategic plan. • Fact-based improvement process.	• Current performance is good to excellent in most areas. • Performance evaluated against competitive comparisons and benchmarks.
	60%	• A sound, systematic approach and deployment in primary areas of organization. • More emphasis is placed on improvement than on reaction to problems.	• Improvement trends reported in many or most areas.
	40%	• No main gaps in deployment. • A sounder, systematic approach.	• Improvement trends reported in some areas.
	20%	• Major gaps in deployment. • Beginning of a systematic approach. • No systematic approach is evident.	• Few or no results reported. • Early stages of developing trends.
Zero Based	0%		

SCORING PROFILES
(Each of the seven Baldrige categories
are profiled into five percentile ranges.)

1.0 Leadership (90 points)

100 - 80%

- Senior executives and health care staff leaders are visibly involved in total quality management.
- Senior leaders are involved and encourage teams to be formed throughout the organization and to focus on continuous improvement.
- Senior leadership communicates organization's quality policies and vision with employees, patients, stakeholders, and suppliers.
- Senior leadership advocates participative management throughout the organization.
- Senior leadership reflects commitment to public health, safety, environmental protection, organizational values, and continuous improvement efforts.

80 - 60%

- Most senior executives and health care staff leaders are visibly involved in promoting quality throughout the organization.
- Senior leaders meet with employee groups/teams, critical suppliers, and patients/stakeholders on quality issues.
- Commitment to public responsibility and organizational citizenship is deployed throughout the organization by senior leaders.
- Management behavior at all levels of the organization reflect quality as a major priority for the organization.
- Senior leaders communicate the organization's quality values, vision, and mission to employees, suppliers, and patients/stakeholders.

60 - 40%

- Senior executives and health care staff leaders share quality values with employees, patients/stakeholders, and suppliers.
- Managers' performance is evaluated against measurable quality strategies.
- Senior leaders committed to public responsibility and corporate citizenship.
- Participative management practiced in many parts of the organization.
- Senior leaders support short- and long-term strategic quality improvement.

40 - 20%

- A few senior executives and health care staff leaders support and are involved in the organization's quality improvement efforts.

- Managers and supervisors are encouraged to become involved in organization's quality improvement efforts.
- Communication within the organization is usually vertical (top-down), no cooperation across departments is encouraged.
- Organization's quality policies reflect commitment to public responsibility and corporate citizenship.
- Continuous improvement is practiced in some parts of the organization.

20 - 0%

- Senior executives and health care staff leaders are beginning to support the quality process.
- Quality practices are not understood in some parts of the organization.
- Senior leaders have not fully developed their quality vision, nor is there a quality plan in place.
- Senior leadership does not get involved with suppliers, patients/stakeholders, and employees in sharing the organization's quality vision.
- Public responsibility and corporate citizenship is of no concern to senior leadership.

2.0 Information and Analysis (75 points)

100 - 80%

- Critical processes data are used to produce and support organizational performance excellence.
- Processes and technology that ensure timely, accurate, valid, and useful data collection for process owners are used throughout the organization.
- Data are analyzed organizationwide by employee teams that translate them into actionable information to ensure continuous quality improvement and performance excellence.
- Competitive comparisons and benchmarking information and data are used to help drive process improvement.
- Quality-related data are integrated and distributed to process owners throughout the organization.

80 - 60%

- Employees have rapid access to data in most parts of the organization.
- Processes and technologies are used across most of the organization to ensure that data are complete, timely, accurate, valid, and useful.
- Comparative data are collected, analyzed, and translated into actionable information to support decision making and planning.
- Most critical processes collect data on quality, timeliness, and productivity.
- Measures exist that relate to the organization's strategic objectives for both clinical and business and support services.

60 - 40%

- Benchmark and comparative data are collected on some clinical, business and support services, and processes.
- Processes and technologies are used across many parts of the organization that ensure data are complete, timely, accurate, valid, and useful.
- Employees have access to data in many parts of the organization.
- Data are collected within many critical processes regarding quality, timeliness, and productivity.
- Measures exist that relate to the organization's strategic objectives for many clinical, business, and support services.

40 - 20%

- Data exist for some critical clinical, business and support services, and processes.
- Data are limited on many major processes.
- Data are collected on some patients/stakeholders and suppliers.
- Centralized group analyzes data, employee teams are not used for data analysis.
- Limited process controls are in place to assure that data analysis is used to drive improvement within the organization.

20 - 0%

- Data received for comparison appear anecdotal.
- Data received are used primarily for reporting purposes, not for improvement.
- Limited data exist for a select few critical processes.
- None or very little patient/stakeholder or supplier data are used for improvement.
- Data analysis is in beginning stages of use for the organization's improvement efforts.

3.0 Strategic Planning (55 points)

100 - 80%

- Strategic planning is used to develop quality improvement goals throughout the organization.
- All employee levels give input to strategic planning process.
- Employees, various patient/stakeholder groups, and suppliers are fully involved in planning process.
- All management levels' activity is involved in planning process.
- Strategic planning process includes short-term and long-term plans based on key quality data, patient/stakeholder and employee survey data, supplier and benchmark data that are deployed throughout the organization.

80 - 60%

- Strategic plans for quality improvement relating to mission, vision, and values are established across the organization.
- Organization uses a broad planning process that involves employees, patients/stakeholders, and suppliers.
- Strategic planning process includes short-term and long-term plans based on key quality data, patient/stakeholder and employee survey data, supplier and benchmark data that are deployed throughout the organization.
- Senior management provides input and approves strategic plan.
- Operational plans are developed throughout the organization that are linked to the master strategic plan; managers are held accountable for meeting strategic goals.

60 - 40%

- Operational plans are developed at key suborganizational levels that link with the strategic plan.
- Managers at all levels are held accountable for obtaining major objectives.
- Organization involves employees, suppliers, and key patient/stakeholder groups in the planning process.
- Strategic planning process includes short-term and long-term plans based on some quality data, patient/stakeholder and employee survey data, supplier and benchmark data that are deployed throughout most parts of the organization.
- Strategic planning process is deployed across the organization and approved by senior management.

40 - 20%

- Strategic goals are established for key functional areas of the organization.
- A strategic planning process is in place within the organization.
- Senior executives approve strategic plan.
- Some patient/stakeholder groups and suppliers are involved in strategic planning process.
- Management provides patient/stakeholder data for the strategic planning process.

20 - 0%

- None to very few patient/stakeholder groups or suppliers are involved in the organization's strategic planning process.
- Personnel at lower levels of organization are not involved in planning process.
- Strategic planning is not mentioned or understood throughout the organization.
- The organization's plan is developed by senior staff with no input from employees, suppliers, or patients/stakeholders.
- The strategic plan has no patient/stakeholder involvement or focus.

4.0 Human Resource Development and Management (140 points)

100 - 80%

- Organization has fully implemented and deployed staff growth and development plans, education, training, and empowerment with measurable results.
- Organization has documented favorable trends regarding percentage of employees recognized for individual and team contributions. Recognition is tied to the organization's quality goals and strategic plan.
- Positive trends with team involvement exist within past few years regarding improved work processes across the organization.
- Employee innovations, cross-functional teams, and natural work groups are encouraged throughout the organization.
- Organization is highly sensitive to employee well-being and satisfaction.

80 - 60%

- Senior leadership and most middle management support employee involvement, contributions, and teamwork.
- Teams and employee work groups feel a strong sense of empowerment and practice innovations across most parts of the organization.
- Employees have rapid access to data through their computer networks in most parts of the organization.
- Employee idea sharing is encouraged and acted upon by management across most parts of the organization.
- Organization maintains a work environment conducive to the well-being and growth of most employees.

60 - 40%

- Employees are empowered throughout many parts of the organization and encouraged to become members of cross-functional and problem-solving teams.
- Organization has a documented strategic plan in place for employee development, education, and skills training.
- Employee recognition is tied to organization's quality goals and objectives.
- Managers in many parts of the organization support teams and team development.
- Organization is sensitive to employee well-being and morale.

40 - 20%

- Employee empowerment is not encouraged throughout the organization.
- Rewards and recognition are not fully deployed among all employee levels; more focused on individual, as opposed to team contributions.

- Not all employee development and training initiatives connected with organization's quality plans and objectives.
- Managers in some parts of the organization support employee involvement and empowerment.
- Organization is not consistently supportive of a work environment conducive to the well-being and growth of employees.

20 - 0%

- Organization does not offer training on a consistent basis.
- Few employees are empowered or work in teams within the organization.
- Employee rewards and recognition appear not to be focused on the organization's quality plan and goals for continuous improvement.
- Employee development is not a priority initiative within the organization.
- Some managers support employee involvement and participative management.

5.0 Process Management (140 points)

100 - 80%

- Work processes are documented and controlled across the organization.
- Systematic approaches are used throughout the organization to ensure shortened cycle time and consistent services.
- Critical supplier partnerships are formed or supplier certification programs are in place to ensure consistency of all processes throughout the organization.
- Periodic assessments of critical processes are conducted.
- Analytic problem-solving tools are used throughout the organization to identify and solve process problems.

80 - 60%

- Processes are documented and controlled across most parts of the organization.
- Systematic approaches are used throughout most parts of the organization to ensure shortened cycle time and consistent services.
- Supplier quality is a main consideration when selecting critical suppliers.
- Comprehensive assessments are conducted consistently throughout the organization to ensure that all processes are meeting patient/stakeholder requirements.
- Analytic problem-solving tools are used in most parts of the organization to identify and solve process problems.

60 - 40%

- Organization uses patient/stakeholder data (i.e., survey data, focus groups) to design processes for new/improved services in many parts of the organization.

- Critical suppliers are required to meet documented standards in many parts of the organization.
- Problem-solving tools are used in many parts of the organization.
- Process assessments are conducted in many parts of the organization.
- Standardized preventative measures to assure quality services are used in many parts of the organization.

40 - 20%

- In most parts of the organization appraisal is emphasized as opposed to prevention.
- Cost is a primary consideration in choosing suppliers.
- Quality assessments of core processes are conducted only when processes are out of control on a consistent basis.
- Problem-solving tools are used in some parts of the organization.
- Some patient/stakeholder input is sought to improve processes.

20 - 0%

- Systematic approaches to ensure reduced cycle time and improved processes are delegated to a single department.
- No patient/stakeholder or supplier input is sought to improve the organization's core processes.
- Suppliers are not considered partners in quality within the organization.
- Very few or no problem-solving tools are used to identify and solve process problems.
- Organization is in appraisal mode versus prevention mode.

6.0 Organizational Performance Results (250 points)

100 - 80%

- Patient/stakeholder satisfaction surveys show positive trends over the past two to three years.
- Supplier data shows improvement over the past two to three years.
- Positive results are shown across the organization in reduced cycle time and productivity improvement within key patient care areas and services over the past two to three years.
- Improvement plans are in place in areas of the organization that show negative trends.
- Patient care support services and community health services show improved results and positive trends over the past two to three years.

80 - 60%

- Most operational performance levels demonstrate positive results over the past two to three years.

- Results indicate some organizational suppliers have improved over the past two to three years.
- Results reflect improvement in cycle time and operational performance.
- Benchmarking results reveal that the organization is leading other health care providers in several core processes.
- Key measures of patient care areas, patient care support areas, and community health services reflect principal quality, productivity, cycle time, and cost results have improved over the past two to three years in most parts of the organization.

60 - 40%

- Patient/stakeholder satisfaction surveys reflect positive results over the past two to three years.
- Critical organizational suppliers are meeting quality standards with a few showing positive results over the past two years.
- Comparisons and benchmarks are conducted within key areas of the organization and benchmark results are documented.
- Key measures of operational and service results are captured in critical areas of the organization. Positive results are reflected over the past two to three years.
- Competitive comparisons are made within the organization that reflect positive one to two year results.

40 - 20%

- Key patient care areas, patient care support service quality, and community health service measures reflect improved trends.
- Patient/stakeholder satisfaction surveys reflect improvement.
- Some suppliers are meeting the organization's documented quality standards.
- Improved results in cycle time and improved patient care services are documented in some parts of the organization.
- Measurement is not fully deployed across the organization.

20 - 0%

- Only anecdotal evidence of improvement exists.
- Patient/stakeholder satisfaction is not measured.
- Improvements are measured in few, if any, parts of the organization.
- Supplier improvement is not measured or considered.
- No benchmarking or comparisons are conducted.

7.0 Focus on and Satisfaction of Patients and Other Stakeholders (250 points)

100 - 80%

- Organization has an effective follow-up process for patients and stakeholders.

- Patient/stakeholder surveys, focus groups, and exit interviews are used to determine satisfaction, loyalty, and referrals relative to competitors.
- Patient/stakeholder relationship training is required throughout the organization for employees who interface with patients/stakeholders.
- Organization promotes trust and confidence in its services.
- Organization is continuously determining short-term and long-term patient/stakeholder requirements and expectations.

80 - 60%

- Effective feedback systems are in place to obtain critical patient/stakeholder data for continuous improvement.
- Senior managers are approachable for patients/stakeholders.
- Specific patient/stakeholder contact training is in place.
- Logistical support is in place for patient/stakeholder contact employees.
- Organization determines short-term and long-term requirements and expectations in most patient care, patient care support services, and community health services.

60 - 40%

- Patient/stakeholder survey data are deployed throughout the organization to drive continuous improvement in services.
- Patient/stakeholder contact employees are trained.
- Customer/stakeholder focus and satisfaction issues tie in with the organization's short-term and long-term strategic plans.
- Effective system is in place to monitor patient/stakeholder satisfaction results within most patient health care services.
- Organization determines short-term and long-term requirements and expectation in many patient care services, patient care support services, and community health services.

40 - 20%

- Some patient/stakeholder groups are segmented.
- Patient/stakeholder service standards are revised periodically for some services.
- Senior management is not always accessible to patients/stakeholders.
- Future patient/stakeholder expectations are not determined or considered in the organization's short-term and long-term planning process.

20 - 0%

- Few, if any, patient/stakeholder service standards have been established by the organization.
- Patient/stakeholder service focus is on problem solving.

- Patient/stakeholder feedback is not always considered when developing or improving services.
- Patient/stakeholder complaints are a major method for obtaining feedback.
- Organization does not promote trust and confidence in its services.

Part II The Baldrige Categories Incorporating Joint Commission Standards

CHAPTER THREE

Category 1.0 Leadership

1.0 Leadership (90 points)

The *Leadership* Category examines senior executives' and health care staff leaders' personal leadership and involvement in creating and sustaining a focus on patient care and organizational mission, clear values and expectations, and a leadership system that promotes quality health care services and performance excellence. Also examined is how the mission, values, and expectations are integrated into the management system, including how the organization addresses its public responsibilities and citizenship.

1.1 NOTES

1.1 Senior Executive and Health Care Staff Leadership (45 points)

Describe senior executives' and health care staff leaders' personal leadership and involvement in setting directions and in developing and maintaining a leadership system for delivering quality health care and performance excellence.

AREAS TO ADDRESS

a. how senior executives and health care staff leaders provide effective coordination, leadership, and direction in building and improving delivery of health care, organizational performance, and capabilities. Describe their roles in: (1) creating and reinforcing mission, values, and expectations throughout the administrative and health care staff leadership systems; (2) creating and sustaining a focus on patients; (3) setting directions and health care and performance excellence goals through strategic and business planning; and (4) reviewing overall performance, including all stakeholders' interests and operational performance.

b. how senior executives and health care staff leaders evaluate and improve the effectiveness of the leadership system and the organization to pursue a focus on patients and health care and performance excellence goals.

1.1 MBNQA Average Percent Score

☑ Approach   ☑ Deployment   ☐ Results

1.1a To what extent do senior executives and health care leaders within your organization personally promote and reinforce a focus on patient care, organizational mission, clear values, and expectations?

Interview notes:

```
                              MBNQA
   Zero-Based                Standards                        World-Class
   ┌────────────────────────────────────────────────────────────────────┐
   │  0    10    20    30    40    50    60    70    80    90    100  │
   └────────────────────────────────────────────────────────────────────┘
              (Circle score that best fits your organization.)
```

Zero-Based Organization

- Not all senior leaders are personally involved in promoting the organization's mission and values throughout the organization and health care staff leadership systems.

- Senior executives and health care leadership do not promote patient focus among the organization's staff.

World-Class Organization

- Senior leaders are personally and visibly involved in promoting a focus on patient care and organizational mission and values among all employees.

- Senior leadership promotes the organization's vision, mission, and core values through in-house videos, speeches, and articles in the employees' newsletter.

☑ Approach   ☑ Deployment   ☐ Results

Examples of Related JCAHO Compliance

Organization's planning (with budgets, resource allocation, and policies); organizational charts including authority statements; mission and vision statements; effective communication of vision and plans deployed throughout organization; plans consider patients needs and satisfaction; essential services are provided in a timely manner; priorities for performance improvement are set.

1.1a   Senior executives and health care leaders' personal promotion of patient focus and organizational excellence.

+ Strengths

1.

2.

3.

- Opportunities for Improvement

1.

2.

3.

Strategic Planning Issues:

    Short Term (1 to 3 years)

    1.

    2.

    Long Term (3 years or more)

    1.

    2.

1.1b How do senior executives and health care leaders evaluate and improve their own leadership effectiveness within your organization?

Interview notes:

MBNQA Standards

Zero-Based   World-Class

| 0 | 10 | 20 | 30 | 40 | 50 | 60 | 70 | 80 | 90 | 100 |

(Circle score that best fits your organization.)

Zero-Based Organization	World-Class Organization

- *Senior leadership does not have a process in place to evaluate and improve their leadership effectiveness.*

- *No process is in place that evaluates how senior executives and health care staff leaders focus on patient care and performance excellence.*

- *Direct report staff rates senior executives and health care staff leaders annually with a leadership questionnaire.*

- *An annual leadership survey is conducted by a third party to evaluate senior leadership effectiveness and their promotion of patient care and service excellence.*

☑ Approach   ☑ Deployment   ☐ Results

Examples of Related JCAHO Compliance

Analysis and assessment of effectiveness of leadership contributions to improving performance, including medical staff leadership performance, is done.

1.1b   Senior leadership evaluates and improves their leadership effectiveness.

+ Strengths

1.

2.

3.

- Opportunities for Improvement

1.

2.

3.

Strategic Planning Issues:

    Short Term (1 to 3 years)

    1.

    2.

    Long Term (3 years or more)

    1.

    2.

1.2 NOTES

1.2 Leadership System and Organization (25 points)

Describe how the organization's focus on patients and all stakeholders and on performance expectations is integrated into the administrative and health care staff leadership systems and organization.

AREAS TO ADDRESS

a. how the administrative and health care staff leadership, management, and organizational systems focus on patients, other stakeholders, and high performance objectives.

b. how the organization effectively communicates, deploys, and reinforces its mission, values, expectations, and directions throughout the entire staff.

c. how overall organizational, departmental, and work unit performance are reviewed and how the reviews are used to improve the quality of health care and operational performance. Describe the types, frequency, and content of reviews, who conducts them, and how the results are aggregated for decision-making.

1.2 MBNQA Average Percent Score

☑ Approach   ☑ Deployment   ☐ Results

1.2a How does your administrative and health care staff promote excellence through their leadership systems and organization?

Interview notes:

MBNQA Standards

Zero-Based | World-Class

| 0 | 10 | 20 | 30 | 40 | 50 | 60 | 70 | 80 | 90 | 100 |

(Circle score that best fits your organization.)

Zero-Based Organization

- *The organization does not focus on patients and other stakeholders when designing new management systems and hiring new managers and executive staff.*

- *The organization's administrative and health care staff leadership systems do not focus on promoting excellence in patient care.*

World-Class Organization

- *The organization has realigned all management positions and organizational systems to focus on improved excellence and cycle time reduction in patient care.*

- *Employee teams are formed within each department to review policies and procedures to ensure that they promote quality health care services and performance excellence.*

☑ Approach ☑ Deployment ☐ Results

Examples of Related JCAHO Compliance

Approach is planned, systematic, and organizationwide, and includes all appropriate departments collaboratively; improvement activities are designed, measured, and assessed.

1.2a   Promotion of patient and stakeholder excellence through leadership systems and organization.

+ Strengths

1.

2.

3.

- Opportunities for Improvement

1.

2.

3.

Strategic Planning Issues:

   Short Term (1 to 3 years)

   1.

   2.

   Long Term (3 years or more)

   1.

   2.

1.2b   How does your organization deploy its mission, values, and expectations to all staff levels?

Interview notes:

MBNQA Standards

Zero-Based ──────────────────────────── World-Class

| 0 | 10 | 20 | 30 | 40 | 50 | 60 | 70 | 80 | 90 | 100 |

(Circle score that best fits your organization.)

Zero-Based Organization

- *Senior leaders seldom reinforce the organization's mission and values to staff throughout the organization.*

- *Senior leaders seldom communicate the organization's mission, values, and expectations to physicians, volunteers, and health profession students.*

World-Class Organization

- *All paid staff, independent practitioners (e.g., physicians) volunteers and health profession students are given a two-hour orientation of the organization's mission, values, and expectations.*

- *Senior executives host luncheons with various staff members each month to promote the organization's patient and stakeholder focus, mission, values, and expectations.*

☑ Approach   ☑ Deployment   ☐ Results

Examples of Related JCAHO Compliance

Organization's mission and plans are communicated to all members of the organization and medical staff.

1.2b   Deployment of mission, values, and expectations to all staff levels.

+ Strengths

1.

2.

3.

- Opportunities for Improvement

1.

2.

3.

Strategic Planning Issues:

   Short Term (1 to 3 years)

   1.

   2.

   Long Term (3 years or more)

   1.

   2.

1.2c How does your organization review overall performance and use this data for improvement?

Interview notes:

MBNQA
Zero-Based **Standards** World-Class

| 0 | 10 | 20 | 30 | 40 | 50 | 60 | 70 | 80 | 90 | 100 |

(Circle score that best fits your organization.)

Zero-Based Organization

- Organization does not consistently review work unit quality and operational performance.

- Accreditation and assessment findings are not consistently reviewed and used to improve the quality of health care and operational performance.

World-Class Organization

- Staff involvement in reviewing accreditation and assessment findings and incorporating the findings into improved performance is widespread throughout the organization.

- Process assessments are conducted annually within each work area and incorporated into improved performance.

✓ Approach ✓ Deployment ☐ Results

Examples of Related JCAHO Compliance

Expectations and plans to improve performance are developed; information systems are available to support collecting, managing, and analyzing data for improvement activities; performance is assessed systematically; medical staff performance is assessed and incorporated into improvement activities.

1.2c   Organization's overall performance review.

+ Strengths

1.

2.

3.

- Opportunities for Improvement

1.

2.

3.

Strategic Planning Issues:

    Short Term (1 to 3 years)

    1.

    2.

    Long Term (3 years or more)

    1.

    2.

1.3 NOTES

1.3 Public Responsibility and Citizenship (20 points)

Describe how the organization includes its responsibilities to the public in its performance improvement practices. Describe also how the organization leads and contributes as a citizen in its key communities.

AREAS TO ADDRESS

a. how the organization includes its public responsibilities into its health care and performance improvement efforts. Describe: (1) the risks and regulatory and other legal requirements addressed in planning and setting health care and operational requirements and targets; (2) how the organization looks ahead to anticipate public concerns and to assess its possible impact in addressing these concerns; and (3) how the organization promotes legal and ethical conduct in all that it does.

b. how the organization leads as a citizen in its key communities. Include a brief summary of the types of leadership and involvement the organization emphasizes.

1.3 MBNQA Average Percent Score

☑ Approach   ☑ Deployment   ☐ Results

1.3a How does your organization integrate its responsibilities to the public in its health care performance improvement practices? (e.g., environment, safety, and emergency preparedness as they relate to risk or adverse effects on the community.)

Interview notes:

MBNQA
Zero-Based **Standards** World-Class

| 0 | 10 | 20 | 30 | 40 | 50 | 60 | 70 | 80 | 90 | 100 |

(Circle score that best fits your organization.)

Zero-Based Organization

- *Organization does not promote environmental, safety, and emergency preparedness above minimum law or regulation requirements.*

- *Organization has no plans in place to coordinate environmental, safety, and emergency preparedness with other community organizations.*

World-Class Organization

- *Organization has an emergency plan in place to coordinate any community disaster with the local health department and Red Cross.*

- *Organization publishes a document that explains its ethical responsibilities to patients and how each responsibility will be addressed.*

☑ Approach   ☑ Deployment   ☐ Results

Examples of Related JCAHO Compliance

Community leaders are involved in planning services; services meet patient needs; applicable laws and regulations are followed; recommendations from authorized planning, regulatory, and inspecting agencies are considered and followed, as appropriate; emergencies are anticipated and drills are conducted; hazardous wastes are handled properly; research is monitored for safety; organ donation plans are developed.

1.3a   Organization's integration of its public responsibilities into its health care and performance improvement practices.

+ Strengths

1.

2.

3.

- Opportunities for Improvement

1.

2.

3.

Strategic Planning Issues:

   Short Term (1 to 3 years)

      1.

      2.

   Long Term (3 years or more)

      1.

      2.

1.3b   Is your organization a leading corporate citizen within your community?

Interview notes:

MBNQA Standards

Zero-Based — World-Class

| 0 | 10 | 20 | 30 | 40 | 50 | 60 | 70 | 80 | 90 | 100 |

(Circle score that best fits your organization.)

Zero-Based Organization

- *Organization has received numerous malpractice lawsuits against several physicians within the past year.*

- *Organization has received several sanctions against patient health care services during the past year.*

World-Class Organization

- *Organization surveys segments of the community to determine how its services contribute to improved community health.*

- *Organization monitors annually its impact on strengthening community health services, education, and environmental management practices.*

☑ Approach   ☑ Deployment   ☐ Results

Examples of Related JCAHO Compliance

Establishing a code of ethical behavior; providing a safe environment; nonsmoking policies are developed.

1.3b Organization's leadership as a corporate citizen within the community.

+ Strengths

1.

2.

3.

- Opportunities for Improvement

1.

2.

3.

Strategic Planning Issues:

　　Short Term (1 to 3 years)

　　1.

　　2.

　　Long Term (3 years or more)

　　1.

　　2.

CHAPTER FOUR

Category 2.0
Information and Analysis

2.0 Information and Analysis (75 points)

The *Information and Analysis* Category examines the management and effectiveness of the use of data and information to support organizational performance excellence as a health care provider and as a business enterprise.

2.1 NOTES

2.1 Management of Information and Data (20 points)

Describe the organization's selection and management of information and data used for planning, management, and evaluation of overall performance as a health care provider and as a business enterprise.

AREAS TO ADDRESS

a. how information and data needed to drive improvement of overall performance as a health care provider and as a business enterprise are selected, integrated, and managed. Describe: (1) the main types of data and information and how each type is related to the key drivers of organizational performance; and (2) how key requirements such as reliability, rapid access, standardization, and rapid update are derived from user needs.

b. how the organization evaluates and improves the selection, analysis, and **integration** of information and data, aligning them with the organization's health care and business needs and priorities. Describe how the evaluation considers: (1) scope of information and data; (2) use and analysis of information and data to support process management and performance improvement; and (3) feedback from users of information and data.

2.1 MBNQA Average Percent Score

☑ Approach   ☑ Deployment   ☐ Results

2.1a How does your organization select, manage, and integrate information and data that it uses for overall performance?

Interview notes:

	MBNQA	
Zero-Based	**Standards**	World-Class

| 0 | 10 | 20 | 30 | 40 | 50 | 60 | 70 | 80 | 90 | 100 |

(Circle score that best fits your organization.)

Zero-Based Organization

- *No selection process is in place to manage and integrate information and data to drive improvement of overall performance.*

- *Organization does not consider user needs of internal customers, patients, and overall stakeholders when selecting information and data for performance improvement.*

World-Class Organization

- *Organization selects and integrates patient care, finance and accounting, marketing, and community health service data to determine overall performance of key programs.*

- *Organization selects, manages, and integrates data within each key program into 12 Service Quality Indicators to help gauge overall organizational performance.*

☑ Approach ☑ Deployment ☐ Results

Examples of Related JCAHO Compliance

Comprehensive assessment and planning of information needs; information security (confidentiality) is maintained; data to be analyzed are identified; uniform data definitions are used; data are collected in a timely, economical, and efficient manner; data are reviewed for completeness, accuracy and timeliness; decision makers are educated in managing information; external databases are available for comparison with internal data; an individual medical record is maintained for each patient; data aggregation is available to support management decisions; providing knowledge-based information as needed to improve care; performance data are collected.

2.1a Organization's selection, management, and integration of information for overall performance.

+ Strengths

1.

2.

3.

- Opportunities for Improvement

1.

2.

3.

Strategic Planning Issues:

   Short Term (1 to 3 years)

   1.

   2.

   Long Term (3 years or more)

   1.

   2.

2.1b How does your organization evaluate and improve its selection, analysis, and integration of information and data used for overall performance?

Interview notes:

Zero-Based   **MBNQA Standards**   **World-Class**

| 0 | 10 | 20 | 30 | 40 | 50 | 60 | 70 | 80 | 90 | 100 |

(Circle score that best fits your organization.)

Zero-Based Organization

- Organization does not evaluate and improve its selection, analysis, and integration of information and data used to drive overall performance.

- Organization does not survey users of data to determine if the data are user friendly and are being used within their work areas for process improvement.

World-Class Organization

- Users of data within all key programs are brought together annually to evaluate the organization's selection, analysis, and integration of information and data used to drive overall performance.

- Organization surveys users to determine if they need training to better use data provided them for process improvement within their work areas.

[✓] Approach   [✓] Deployment   [ ] Results

Examples of Related JCAHO Compliance

Information management processes are based on a comprehensive assessment of needs.

Information and Analysis 53

2.1b   Organization's evaluation and improvement of its selection, analysis, and integration of data.

+ Strengths

1.

2.

3.

- Opportunities for Improvement

1.

2.

3.

Strategic Planning Issues:

   Short Term (1 to 3 years)

   1.

   2.

   Long Term (3 years or more)

   1.

   2.

2.2 NOTES

2.2 Performance Comparisons and Benchmarking (15 points)

Describe the organization's processes for obtaining and its uses of comparative information and data to support improvement of overall performance as a health care provider and as a business enterprise.

AREAS TO ADDRESS

a. how competitive comparisons and benchmarking information and data are selected and used to help drive improvement of overall organizational performance as a health care provider and as a business enterprise. Describe: (1) how needs and priorities are determined; (2) criteria for seeking appropriate information and data on delivery of health care services, and sources for the information and data; (3) criteria for seeking appropriate information and data on administrative and business functions, using sources from within and outside the health care provider industry; (4) how the information and data are used and integrated within the organization to improve understanding of processes and process performance; and (5) how the information and data are used to set stretch targets and/or encourage breakthrough approaches.

b. how the organization evaluates and improves its overall process for selecting, using, and **integrating** competitive comparisons and benchmarking information and data to improve planning and overall organizational performance.

2.2 MBNQA Average Percent Score

✓ Approach   ✓ Deployment   ☐ Results

2.2a How does your organization select and use comparison and benchmark data to drive improvement and operational performance?

Interview notes:

```
                              MBNQA
    Zero-Based               Standards                        World-Class
    | 0   10   20   30   40   50   60   70   80   90   100 |
              (Circle score that best fits your organization.)
```

Zero-Based Organization

- *No comparisons and benchmarks are conducted to drive improvement and operational performance.*

- *Comparison and benchmark data are not selected and used for operational improvements in units/departments.*

World-Class Organization

- *Comparisons and benchmarks are conducted throughout the organization to improve units'/departments' overall performance.*

- *Comparisons and benchmarks are identified and selected against "best practices" of other health care providers and organizations to set stretch targets and goals within units/departments.*

[✓] Approach   [✓] Deployment   [ ] Results

Examples of Related JCAHO Compliance

Use of external databases for comparisons; indicators are used to assess processes and outcomes; performance is evaluated against practice guidelines and relevant scientific, clinical, and management literature; statistical process control techniques are used.

2.2a   Organization's selection and use of comparisons and benchmark data for operational improvement.

+ Strengths

1.

2.

3.

- Opportunities for Improvement

1.

2.

3.

Strategic Planning Issues:

    Short Term (1 to 3 years)

        1.

        2.

    Long Term (3 years or more)

        1.

        2.

2.2b How does your organization evaluate the scope and validity of your comparison and benchmark process to improve planning and operational performance?

Interview notes:

	MBNQA Standards	
Zero-Based		World-Class

```
0    10    20    30    40    50    60    70    80    90    100
```

(Circle score that best fits your organization.)

Zero-Based Organization

- *Organization provides no information or training to employees on how to use comparison and benchmark data for process improvement.*

- *Comparison and benchmark data are not used by the organization to set "stretch" goals and to improve planning and operational performance.*

World-Class Organization

- *Organization has published a document that outlines how to conduct comparisons and benchmarks against other health care providers and outside industry organizations.*

- *Comparisons and benchmark data reviewed and evaluated quarterly to improve organizational planning and overall performance.*

☑ Approach   ☑ Deployment   ☐ Results

Examples of Related JCAHO Compliance

A systematic data assessment process is used; performance is evaluated against reference databases and against relevant scientific, clinical, and management literature.

2.2b   Evaluation and improvement of organization's comparison and benchmark process.

+ Strengths

1.

2.

3.

- Opportunities for Improvement

1.

2.

3.

Strategic Planning Issues:

    Short Term (1 to 3 years)

        1.

        2.

    Long Term (3 years or more)

        1.

        2.

2.3 NOTES

2.3 Analysis and Use of Organizational-Level Data (40 points)

Describe how data related to health care and business service quality, patients, other stakeholders, and operational performance, together with relevant financial data, are analyzed to support organizational-level review, action, and planning.

AREAS TO ADDRESS

a. how information and data from all parts of the organization are integrated and analyzed to support reviews, organizational decision making, and planning. Describe how analysis is used to gain understanding of: (1) patients, other stakeholders, health care service quality, and health care markets; (2) operational performance and organizational capabilities; and (3) performance relative to competitors and other organizations delivering similar health care services.

b. how the organization relates patient, other stakeholder, and health care market data, improvements in health care service quality and offerings, and improvements in operational performance to changes in financial and/or health care market indicators of performance. Describe how this information is used to set priorities for health care service and business improvement actions.

2.3 MBNQA Average Percent Score

☑ Approach   ☑ Deployment   ☐ Results

62 THE BALDRIGE WORKBOOK FOR HEALTHCARE

2.3a How are data from all parts of the organization integrated and analyzed to support organizationwide decision making and planning?

Interview notes:

MBNQA
Zero-Based **Standards** World-Class

| 0 | 10 | 20 | 30 | 40 | 50 | 60 | 70 | 80 | 90 | 100 |

(Circle score that best fits your organization.)

Zero-Based Organization

- *Organization does not consistently integrate key data to support overall decision making and planning.*

- *Organization does not analyze and trend data, nor consider correlating data throughout its operation to support decision making and planning.*

World-Class Organization

- *Organization integrates data from areas to support decision making and planning.*

- *Organization correlates key patient/ stakeholder satisfaction data with length of stay, wait time, and delay data to support decision making and planning within various units/departments.*

☑ Approach ☑ Deployment ☐ Results

Examples of Related JCAHO Compliance

Information management processes are planned and designed to meet the health care organization's internal and external needs; reference databases are used; format and methods for disseminating data and information meets user's needs; relevant information is forwarded to appropriate leaders responsible for coordinating organizationwide performance improvement activities; patient satisfaction with services is monitored.

2.3a   Data integration supports organizationwide decision making and planning.

+ Strengths

1.

2.

3.

- Opportunities for Improvement

1.

2.

3.

Strategic Planning Issues:

    Short Term (1 to 3 years)

    1.

    2.

    Long Term (3 years or more)

    1.

    2.

2.3b Does your organization collect key patient, other stakeholder, and health care cost, financial, and market data and translate it into usable information for employees to use to support decision making and improvement?

Interview notes:

MBNQA Standards

Zero-Based ——— World-Class

| 0 | 10 | 20 | 30 | 40 | 50 | 60 | 70 | 80 | 90 | 100 |

(Circle score that best fits your organization.)

Zero-Based Organization

- Data are not used by the organization to support decision making and improvement.

- Data are used only to justify programs to the board of directors, not to support operational decision making and improvement.

World-Class Organization

- Organization sets priorities for health care service and business improvement by using various cost, financial, and market data to support decision making.

- Organization has selected specific cost, financial, and market data to review quarterly to support decisions on providing additional programs and improvement initiatives.

[✓] Approach [✓] Deployment [ ] Results

Examples of Related JCAHO Compliance

The information management function provides for the definition, capture, analysis, transmission, and reporting of data/information that can be aggregated in support of managerial decisions and operations, performance improvement activities, and patient care.

Information and Analysis   65

2.3b   Cost, financial, and market data translated into usable information to support the organization's decision making and improvement.

+ Strengths

1.

2.

3.

- Opportunities for Improvement

1.

2.

3.

Strategic Planning Issues:

   Short Term (1 to 3 years)

   1.

   2.

   Long Term (3 years or more)

   1.

   2.

CHAPTER FIVE

Category 3.0 Strategic Planning

3.0 Strategic Planning (55 points)

The *Strategic Planning* Category examines how the organization sets strategic directions and how it determines key strategic plan requirements. Also examined is how the plan requirements are translated into an effective health care and business performance management system.

3.1 NOTES

3.1 Strategy Development (35 points)

Describe the organization's strategic planning process for overall performance as a health care provider and business enterprise and for short-term and longer-term competitive leadership relative to other organizations providing similar health care services. Describe also how this process leads to the development of key drivers of organizational performance that serve as a basis for deploying plan requirements throughout the organization.

AREAS TO ADDRESS

a. how the organization develops strategies, plans for health care services, and business plans to strengthen its performance as a health care provider and business enterprise. Describe how strategy development considers: (1) patient requirements and expectations and their expected changes; (2) other stakeholder's requirements and expectations and their expected changes; (3) the competitive environment; (4) risks: financial, regulatory, health care market, technological, and societal; (5) organizational capabilities—human resource, technology, research and development, and business/administrative systems and processes—to seek new leadership opportunities, and/or to prepare for key new requirements and operational constraints, and (6) partnering capabilities, including any health care provider alliances.

b. how strategies and plans are translated into actionable key drivers of organizational performance that serve as the basis for deploying plan requirements, addressed in Item 3.2.

c. how the organization evaluates and improves its strategic planning and plan deployment processes.

3.1 MBNQA Average Percent Score

☑ Approach   ☑ Deployment   ☐ Results

3.1a How is your organization's overall strategic planning process integrated with patient and other stakeholder requirements, market share issues, financial and regulatory risks, organizational capabilities, health care partnerships and alliances ensuring competitive leadership?

Interview notes:

MBNQA Standards

Zero-Based   World-Class

| 0 | 10 | 20 | 30 | 40 | 50 | 60 | 70 | 80 | 90 | 100 |

(Circle score that best fits your organization.)

Zero-Based Organization

- Organization does not consider competitive factors when developing its organizational strategies and business plans.

- Organization's strategy development does not consider patient and stakeholder requirements, market share issues, financial and regulatory risks when developing its strategies and business plan.

World-Class Organization

- Organization's overall strategies and business plans address short- and long-term competitive leadership initiatives relative to other organizations providing similar health care services.

- Patients' and other stakeholders' input along with competitive, financial, and community data help determine the organization's strategic directions.

☑ Approach   ☑ Deployment   ☐ Results

Examples of Related JCAHO Compliance

Evidence indicates a high correlation between the content of the mission statement and the content of long-range, strategic and operational plans, budgets, resource allocation and policies; services are designed to be responsive to the needs and expectations of patients and/or families/decision makers; when appropriate, community leaders are involved in planning services.

3.1a Organization's integration of its strategic planning process ensures competitive leadership.

+ Strengths

1.

2.

3.

- Opportunities for Improvement

1.

2.

3.

Strategic Planning Issues:

   Short Term (1 to 3 years)

     1.

     2.

   Long Term (3 years or more)

     1.

     2.

3.1b How does your organization translate and deploy key strategies and plans into actionable performance improvements?

Interview notes:

MBNQA Standards

Zero-Based — World-Class

| 0 | 10 | 20 | 30 | 40 | 50 | 60 | 70 | 80 | 90 | 100 |

(Circle score that best fits your organization.)

Zero-Based Organization

- Strategies and the business plan are shared throughout the organization, but no actionable initiatives are developed throughout the organization.

- Organization's strategies and business plan are not shared beyond senior management levels.

World-Class Organization

- Organization shares strategic plan with all employees and requires that actionable initiatives be developed within each department.

- Quarterly reviews are conducted within each department to check progress against strategies and the business plan.

☑ Approach   ☑ Deployment   ☐ Results

Examples of Related JCAHO Compliance

The organization has a planned, organizationwide approach to designing, measuring, assessing, and improving its performance; all appropriate departments are involved in the design, measurement, assessment, and improvement activities.

3.1b   Strategies and plans translated and deployed into actionable improvements.

+ Strengths

1.

2.

3.

- Opportunities for Improvement

1.

2.

3.

Strategic Planning Issues:

    Short Term (1 to 3 years)

        1.

        2.

    Long Term (3 years or more)

        1.

        2.

3.1c Is your organization's strategic planning and plan deployment evaluated and improved continuously?

Interview notes:

	MBNQA	
Zero-Based	**Standards**	World-Class

| 0 | 10 | 20 | 30 | 40 | 50 | 60 | 70 | 80 | 90 | 100 |

(Circle score that best fits your organization.)

Zero-Based Organization

- *Organization's planning process is driven by senior leadership and not reviewed for improvement.*

- *Organization does not evaluate and improve its strategic planning process and plan deployment.*

World-Class Organization

- *Each department plans and gives input to the organization's strategic plan; work units review planning process annually for improvement.*

- *Each work area has strategic objectives listed and quarterly reviews are conducted throughout the organization.*

☑ Approach ☑ Deployment ☐ Results

Examples of Related JCAHO Compliance

The planning process provides for setting the organization's priorities for performance improvement, including mechanisms designed to reprioritize in response to unusual or urgent events.

3.1c   Strategic plans and plan deployment evaluated and improved continuously.

+ Strengths

1.

2.

3.

- Opportunities for Improvement

1.

2.

3.

Strategic Planning Issues:

    Short Term (1 to 3 years)

        1.

        2.

    Long Term (3 years or more)

        1.

        2.

3.2 NOTES

3.2 Strategy Deployment (20 points)

Summarize the key drivers of organizational performance and how they are deployed. Show how the organization's performance projects into the future relative to the competitive environment and key benchmarks.

> **AREAS TO ADDRESS**
>
> **a.** summary of the specific key drivers of organizational performance derived from the organization's strategic directions and how these drivers are translated into an action plan. Describe: (1) key performance requirements and associated performance measures and/or indicators and how they are deployed; (2) how the organization aligns plans for health care services and business plans; (3) how the organization aligns work unit/departmental plans and how these plans are aligned with supplier and/or partner plans and targets; (4) how productivity and cycle time improvement and reduction in waste are included in plans and targets; and (5) the principal resources committed to the accomplishment of plans. Note any important distinctions between short-term plans and longer-term plans.
>
> **b.** two-to-five year projection of key measures and/or indicators of the organization's patient-related, stakeholder-related, and operational performance. Describe how patient care service quality and operational performance might be expected to compare over this time period to key competitors, other organizations providing similar health care services, and key benchmarks. Briefly explain the comparisons, including estimates or assumptions made regarding projected patient care service quality and operational performance of competitive/similar health care providers, projected changes in the applicant's health care marketplace, and/or changes in key benchmarks.

3.2 MBNQA Average Percent Score

[✓] Approach   [✓] Deployment   [ ] Results

3.2a How are your organization's short- and long-term operational plans aligned to ensure total integration of organizational performance?

Interview notes:

MBNQA
Zero-Based **Standards** World-Class

| 0 | 10 | 20 | 30 | 40 | 50 | 60 | 70 | 80 | 90 | 100 |

(Circle score that best fits your organization.)

Zero-Based Organization

- *Organization has no alignment of its short- and long-term projects with its strategies and business plan.*

- *No alignment exists between the organization's short- and long-term goals and strategies and each work unit's operational performance.*

World-Class Organization

- *Each department has in place actionable performance goals and strategies that are fully integrated with the organization's short- and long-term strategic plans.*

- *Each manager receives a quarterly update progress report toward meeting his work unit's goals against the organization's strategies and business plan.*

☑ Approach   ☑ Deployment   ☐ Results

Examples of Related JCAHO Compliance

The organization collects data regarding the needs and expectations of patients and others and the degree to which these needs and expectations have been met.

3.2a   Alignment of short- and long-term operational plans.

+ Strengths

1.

2.

3.

- Opportunities for Improvement

1.

2.

3.

Strategic Planning Issues:

    Short Term (1 to 3 years)

    1.

    2.

    Long Term (3 years or more)

    1.

    2.

3.2b How does your organization address two-to-five-year projected performance improvement against key comparisons and benchmarks?

Interview notes:

	MBNQA	
Zero-Based	**Standards**	World-Class

0	10	20	30	40	50	60	70	80	90	100

(Circle score that best fits your organization.)

Zero-Based Organization

- *No competitive benchmarks are made by the organization.*
- *Projected performance improvement is based on anecdotal information shared among senior leadership.*

World-Class Organization

- *Short- and long-term projections are made after competitive and benchmark comparisons are made.*
- *Organization's long-term projections are based on comparisons/benchmarks and competitive marketplace data.*

☑ Approach   ☑ Deployment   ☐ Results

3.2b   Projection two-to-five years in advance of changes in quality levels against key comparisons and benchmarks.

+ Strengths

1.

2.

3.

- Opportunities for Improvement

1.

2.

3.

Strategic Planning Issues:

　　Short Term (1 to 3 years)

　　　1.

　　　2.

　　Long Term (3 years or more)

　　　1.

　　　2.

CHAPTER SIX

Category 4.0 Human Resource Development and Management

4.0 Human Resource Development and Management (140 points)

The *Human Resource Development and Management* Category examines how the organization's entire staff is enabled to develop and utilize its full potential, aligned with the organization's health care and business performance objectives. Also examined are the organization's efforts to build and maintain an environment conducive to performance excellence, full participation by all employees and health care staff, and personal and organizational growth.

4.1 NOTES

4.1 Human Resource Planning and Evaluation (20 points)

Describe how the organization's human resource planning and evaluation are aligned with its strategies, health care and business plans, and address the development and well-being of the entire staff.

AREAS TO ADDRESS

a. how the organization translates overall requirements from planning (Category 3.0) to specific human resource plans. Summarize key human resource plans in the following areas: (1) changes in work process design to improve flexibility, efficiency, coordination, and response time; (2) employee and health care staff development, education, and training, including credentialling needs; (3) changes in compensation, recognition, and benefits; (4) expected or planned changes in the composition of the health care and/or employed staff; and (5) recruitment of new staff. Distinguish between the short term and the longer term, as appropriate.

b. how the organization evaluates and improves its human resource planning and practices, and the alignment of the plans and practices with its health care and business plans. Include how employee and health care staff-related data and organizational performance data are analyzed and used: (1) to assess the development and well-being of all categories and types of staff; (2) to assess the linkage of human resource practices to key organizational performance results (Category 6.0); and (3) to ensure that reliable and complete human resource information is available for health care and business planning.

☐ 4.1 MBNQA Average Percent Score

☑ Approach ☑ Deployment ☐ Results

4.1a Are your organization's human resource plans driven by the goals outlined in your strategic health care and business plans? (e.g., work process redesign, training, development, hiring, employee involvement, empowerment, and recognition.)

Interview notes:

MBNQA Standards

Zero-Based ────────────────── World-Class

| 0 | 10 | 20 | 30 | 40 | 50 | 60 | 70 | 80 | 90 | 100 |

(Circle score that best fits your organization.)

Zero-Based Organization

- *Performance evaluations not written in language to reinforce organization's quality values.*

- *Organization does not have in place a recognition program for paid staff, independent practitioners (e.g., physicians) and volunteers that are strategically aligned with the organization's short- and long-term plans and goals.*

World-Class Organization

- *Human Resource plan integrated with the organization's strategic plan.*

- *Organization has redesigned work processes and jobs to increase staff opportunities, responsibility, decision making, and response time.*

☑ Approach   ☑ Deployment   ☐ Results

Examples of Related JCAHO Compliance

All staff positions throughout the organization have defined qualifications and a system for evaluating job performance; the organization has implemented methods and practices that support self-development, learning, and in-services (educational sessions) for all staff.

Human Resource Development and Management 87

4.1a Human resource plans aligned with organization's strategic health care and business plans.

+ Strengths

1.

2.

3.

- Opportunities for Improvement

1.

2.

3.

Strategic Planning Issues:

    Short Term (1 to 3 years)

    1.

    2.

    Long Term (3 years or more)

    1.

    2.

4.1b Does your organization evaluate and improve its human resource planning and practices on a consistent basis?

Interview notes:

MBNQA Standards

Zero-Based 0 10 20 30 40 50 60 70 80 90 100 World-Class

(Circle score that best fits your organization.)

Zero-Based Organization

- *Human resource planning and evaluation is not driven by employee-related data (e.g., survey data, employee focus group data, etc.).*

- *Human resource planning does not appear to be aligned with the organization's business plan.*

World-Class Organization

- *Organization collects data on turnover, absenteeism, safety, grievances, involvement, recognition, training, and employee exit interviews to drive improvement.*

- *Organization uses an employee satisfaction survey and participative management survey to gauge employee satisfaction.*

☑ Approach   ☑ Deployment   ☐ Results

Examples of Related JCAHO Compliance

Process are designed to ensure that the competence of all staff members is assessed, maintained, demonstrated, and improved on an ongoing basis.

4.1b Human resource plans and practices evaluated and improved on a consistent basis.

+ Strengths

1.

2.

3.

- Opportunities for Improvement

1.

2.

3.

Strategic Planning Issues:

    Short Term (1 to 3 years)

        1.

        2.

    Long Term (3 years or more)

        1.

        2.

4.2 NOTES

4.2 Employee/Health Care Staff Work Systems (45 points)

Describe how the organization's work systems for provision of health care and administrative services and its job design contribute to achieving high performance. Also describe how compensation and/or recognition approaches enable and encourage all staff to contribute effectively.

AREAS TO ADDRESS

a. how the organization's work systems for provision of health care and administrative services and the organization's job design: (1) create opportunities for initiative and self-directed responsibility; (2) foster flexibility, efficiency, improved coordination, and rapid response to changing requirements; and (3) ensure effective communications across functions or units/departments that need to work together to meet patient, other stakeholder, and/or operational requirements.

b. how the organization's compensation and recognition approaches for individuals and groups, including health care staff, reinforce the effectiveness of the work and job design.

4.2 MBNQA Average Percent Score

☑ Approach   ☑ Deployment   ☐ Results

4.2a How does your organization select and use comparison and benchmark data to drive improvement and operational performance?

Interview notes:

                                  MBNQA

Zero-Based   **Standards**   World-Class

0	10	20	30	40	50	60	70	80	90	100

(Circle score that best fits your organization.)

Zero-Based Organization   World-Class Organization

- *No comparisons and benchmarks are conducted to drive improvement and operational performance.*

- *Comparison and benchmark data are not selected and used for operational improvements in units/departments.*

- *Comparisons and benchmarks are conducted throughout the organization to improve units'/departments' overall performance.*

- *Comparisons and benchmarks are identified and selected against "best practices" of other health care providers and organizations to set stretch targets and goals within units/departments.*

☑ Approach   ☑ Deployment   ☐ Results

Examples of Related JCAHO Compliance

The leaders individually and jointly develop and participate in systematic and effective mechanisms designed for fostering communication among individuals and components of the organization and coordinating internal activities. Processes are designed to ensure that the competence of all staff members is assessed, maintained, demonstrated, and improved on an ongoing basis.

4.2a   Design of work systems to better meet patient and stakeholder requirements.

+ Strengths

1.

2.

3.

- Opportunities for Improvement

1.

2.

3.

Strategic Planning Issues:

   Short Term (1 to 3 years)

     1.

     2.

   Long Term (3 years or more)

     1.

     2.

4.2b   Does employee compensation and recognition support your organization's work systems design?

Interview notes:

		MBNQA		
Zero-Based		**Standards**		World-Class

| 0 | 10 | 20 | 30 | 40 | 50 | 60 | 70 | 80 | 90 | 100 |

(Circle score that best fits your organization.)

Zero-Based Organization

- *Organization does not have a formal recognition program in place.*

- *Staff members are penalized for practicing empowerment and innovation.*

World-Class Organization

- *Organization has in place a recognition program that promotes staff empowerment and innovation.*

- *Gain-share and pay-for-knowledge programs promote increased staff involvement in key work processes throughout the organization.*

☑ Approach   ☑ Deployment   ☐ Results

4.2b   Employee compensation and recognition supports organization's work systems design.

+ Strengths

1.

2.

3.

- Opportunities for Improvement

1.

2.

3.

Strategic Planning Issues:

   Short Term (1 to 3 years)

   1.

   2.

   Long Term (3 years or more)

   1.

   2.

4.3 NOTES

4.3 Employee/Health Care Staff Education, Training, and Development (50 points)

Describe how the organization's education and training address organizational needs and plans, including building capabilities and responding to changes in health care delivery. Also describe how the organization's education and training contribute to staff motivation, progression, and development.

AREAS TO ADDRESS

a. how the organization's education and training serve as a key vehicle in building organizational and staff capabilities and in responding to changes in health care delivery. Describe how education and training address: (1) key performance objectives, including those related to enhancing high performance work systems and changes in health care delivery; (2) development of all employees and health care staff; and (3) maintenance of licensure and recredentialling requirements.

b. how education and training are designed, delivered, reinforced, and evaluated. Include: (1) how employees and health care staff contribute to or are involved in determining specific education and training needs and designing education and training; (2) how education and training are delivered; (3) how licensure and recredentialling requirements are translated into educational program designs; (4) how knowledge and skills are reinforced on the job; and (5) how education and training are evaluated and improved.

4.3 MBNQA Average Percent Score

☑ Approach   ☑ Deployment   ☐ Results

4.3a   What methods and indicators are used to ensure that organizational needs and changes within employees' work areas are being addressed through education and training?

Interview notes:

MBNQA Standards

Zero-Based   World-Class

| 0 | 10 | 20 | 30 | 40 | 50 | 60 | 70 | 80 | 90 | 100 |

(Circle score that best fits your organization.)

<u>Zero-Based Organization</u>

- *Organization offers no training beyond what is required by law.*
- *Employee's input is not sought or considered when determining training needs.*

<u>World-Class Organization</u>

- *Organization conducts training needs assessments annually throughout the work force.*
- *Employee focus groups are formed within each department to help determine education and training needs to meet overall work objectives.*

☑ Approach   ☑ Deployment   ☐ Results

Examples of Related JCAHO Compliance

All staff positions throughout the organization have defined qualifications and a system for evaluating job performance; the organization has implemented methods and practices that support self-development learning, and in-service for all staff; processes are designed to ensure that the competence of all staff members, including the medical staff, is assessed, maintained, demonstrated, and improved on an ongoing basis; continuing education activities relate, at least in part, to the type and nature of care offered by the hospital and the findings of performance-improvement activities; the hospital establishes hospital-specific mechanisms for appointing and reappointing medical staff members and for granting and renewing or revising clinical privileges.

4.3a   Organizational needs and changes are being addressed through education and training.

+ Strengths

1.

2.

3.

- Opportunities for Improvement

1.

2.

3.

Strategic Planning Issues:

   Short Term (1 to 3 years)

     1.

     2.

   Long Term (3 years or more)

     1.

     2.

4.3b How is education and training designed, delivered, enforced, and evaluated to ensure staff motivation, progression, and development?

Interview notes:

MBNQA Standards

Zero-Based — World-Class

| 0 | 10 | 20 | 30 | 40 | 50 | 60 | 70 | 80 | 90 | 100 |

(Circle score that best fits your organization.)

Zero-Based Organization

- *No follow-up is conducted to determine if new learning is applied to on-the-job improvement.*

- *No formal process is in place to consistently incorporate changes in health care clinical training programs.*

World-Class Organization

- *After each training program questionnaires are distributed to all participants and their managers to gauge application of new learning to job improvement.*

- *Training is focused and measured against improved job and operational performance improvement targets and results.*

☑ Approach   ☑ Deployment   ☐ Results

Examples of Related JCAHO Compliance

Appointment and reappointment to the medical staff and the initial granting and renewal or revision of clinical privileges are also based on information regarding the applicant's competence; hospital sponsored educational activities relate, at least in part, to the type and nature of care offered by the hospital and the findings of performance-improvement activities; processes are designed to assure that the competence of all staff members is assessed, maintained, demonstrated, and improved on a continuing basis.

4.3b   Design, delivery, and evaluation of education and training supports staff development.

+ Strengths

1.

2.

3.

- Opportunities for Improvement

1.

2.

3.

Strategic Planning Issues:

   Short Term (1 to 3 years)

   1.

   2.

   Long Term (3 years or more)

   1.

   2.

4.4 NOTES

4.4 Employee/Health Care Staff Well-Being and Satisfaction (25 points)

Describe how the organization maintains a work environment and a work climate conducive to the well-being and development of all staff.

AREAS TO ADDRESS

a. how the organization maintains a safe and healthful work environment. Include: (1) how employee/health care staff well-being factors such as health, safety, and ergonomics are included in improvement activities; and (2) principal improvement requirements, measures and/or indicators, and targets for each factor relevant and important to the organization's work environment. Note any significant differences based upon differences in work environments among employees and health care staff.

b. what services, facilities, activities, and opportunities the organization makes available to employees and health care staff to support their overall well-being, and satisfaction, and/or to enhance their work experience and development potential.

c. how the organization determines employee/health care staff satisfaction, well-being and motivation. Include a brief description of methods, frequency, the specific factors used in this determination, and how the information is used to improve satisfaction, well-being, and motivation. Note any important differences in methods or factors used for different categories or types of staff, as appropriate.

4.4 MBNQA Average Percent Score

☑ Approach   ☑ Deployment   ☐ Results

4.4a Does your organization constantly work on projects to improve safety, health, ergonomics, employee morale, and job satisfaction?

Interview notes:

MBNQA
Zero-Based **Standards** World-Class

| 0 | 10 | 20 | 30 | 40 | 50 | 60 | 70 | 80 | 90 | 100 |

(Circle score that best fits your organization.)

Zero-Based Organization

- *Ergonomics is not addressed by the organization.*

- *Senior leadership is not aware of employee morale and satisfaction issues.*

World-Class Organization

- *Personal and career counseling is available for staff.*

- *Employee safety and health issues are viewed as paramount in importance to organization.*

☑ Approach   ☑ Deployment   ☐ Results

Examples of Related JCAHO Compliance

The organization designs a safe, accessible, effective, and efficient environment of care in accordance with its mission and services, as well as applicable laws and regulations; the organization has documented management plans for the environment of care that considers the following factors: safety, security, hazardous materials and waste, emergency preparedness, life safety, medical equipment, and utility systems; there is implementation of strategies to reduce risks for nosocomial infections in employees.

4.4a   Organization's maintenance of a safe and healthful work environment.

+ Strengths

1.

2.

3.

- Opportunities for Improvement

1.

2.

3.

Strategic Planning Issues:

   Short Term (1 to 3 years)

   1.

   2.

   Long Term (3 years or more)

   1.

   2.

4.4b What services, facilities, activities, and opportunities does your organization offer to support overall employee well-being and satisfaction?

Interview notes:

	MBNQA	
Zero-Based	**Standards**	World-Class

| 0 | 10 | 20 | 30 | 40 | 50 | 60 | 70 | 80 | 90 | 100 |

(Circle score that best fits your organization.)

Zero-Based Organization

- *Organization offers limited special services for staff.*

- *Organization has limited recreational facilities and activities for staff.*

World-Class Organization

- *Organization provides special services for the work force that includes day care, special leave for community services, career enhancement activities, and career counseling.*

- *Staff focus groups meet quarterly within each department to discuss work force issues.*

☑ Approach ☑ Deployment ☐ Results

Examples of Related JCAHO Compliance

The organization has established methods and practices that encourage self-development and learning for all staff.

4.4b   Special services, facilities, activities, and opportunities offered to employees.

+ Strengths

1.

2.

3.

- Opportunities for Improvement

1.

2.

3.

Strategic Planning Issues:

    Short Term (1 to 3 years)

        1.

        2.

    Long Term (3 years or more)

        1.

        2.

4.4c How does your organization determine employee satisfaction? (e.g., surveys, employee focus groups, etc.)

Interview notes:

MBNQA
Zero-Based **Standards** World-Class

| 0 | 10 | 20 | 30 | 40 | 50 | 60 | 70 | 80 | 90 | 100 |

(Circle score that best fits your organization.)

Zero-Based Organization

- Employee satisfaction and well-being is not addressed by the organization.

- Organization has no methods in place to determine employee satisfaction.

World-Class Organization

- Regular employee satisfaction survey is conducted.

- Employee focus groups are deployed throughout the organization to discuss and determine employee satisfaction issues.

☑ Approach ☑ Deployment ☐ Results

Examples of Related JCAHO Compliance

The organization collects information about the needs and expectations of patients and others and the degree to which these needs and expectations have been met.

4.4c   Determination of employee satisfaction.

+ Strengths

1.

2.

3.

- Opportunities for Improvement

1.

2.

3.

Strategic Planning Issues:

   Short Term (1 to 3 years)

     1.

     2.

   Long Term (3 years or more)

     1.

     2.

CHAPTER SEVEN

Category 5.0
Process Management

5.0 Process Management (140 points)

The *Process Management* Category examines the key aspects of process management, including design and delivery of patient health care services, patient care support services, community health services, administrative and business support processes, and supplier performance management. Process management involves all aspects of the organization's operations and staff. The Category examines how key processes are designed, effectively managed, and improved to achieve higher performance.

5.1 NOTES

5.1 Design and Introduction of Patient Health Care Services (35 points)

Describe how new and/or modified patient health care services are designed and introduced, and how they are designed to meet key service quality and operational/financial requirements.

AREAS TO ADDRESS

a. how patient health care services are designed. Include how financial considerations are factored into decision-making. Describe: (1) how decisions are made to launch new patient health care services; (2) how patient needs and desires, regulatory and payor requirements, and technological and other innovations are translated into effective and efficient patient health care processes, including appropriate measurement plans for the services; (3) how all delivery requirements associated with the services are addressed early in design by all appropriate organizational units/departments, and suppliers/partners to ensure integration, coordination, and capability.

b. how patient health care service designs are reviewed and/or tested to ensure safe, effective, trouble-free initiation.

c. how service design and design processes are evaluated and improved so that new service initiation is continuously improved. Include the factors considered in evaluations and who conducts the evaluations.

5.1 MBNQA Average Percent Score

☑ Approach ☑ Deployment ☐ Results

5.1a   Are your organization's human resource plans driven by the goals outlined in your strategic health care and business plans? (e.g., work process redesign, training, development, hiring, employee involvement, empowerment, and recognition.)

Interview notes:

MBNQA
Zero-Based   **Standards**   World-Class

| 0 | 10 | 20 | 30 | 40 | 50 | 60 | 70 | 80 | 90 | 100 |

(Circle score that best fits your organization.)

Zero-Based Organization

- *No formal process in place to determine patient and other stakeholder input before designing new health care services.*

- *Design of new programs and services is not based on patient and other stakeholder input.*

World-Class Organization

- *Surveys used to determine patient and other stakeholder requirements.*

- *Patient and other stakeholder focus groups are conducted to provide input before new or modified patient health care services are designed and introduced.*

☑ Approach   ☑ Deployment   ☐ Results

Examples of Related JCAHO Compliance
Services are designed to be responsive to the needs and expectations of patients and/or their families/decision makers; the budget review process includes consideration of the appropriateness of the organization's plan for providing care to meet patient needs.

5.1a   Design of new health care services.

+ Strengths

1.

2.

3.

- Opportunities for Improvement

1.

2.

3.

Strategic Planning Issues:

   Short Term (1 to 3 years)

     1.

     2.

   Long Term (3 years or more)

     1.

     2.

5.1b Describe the overall process your organization uses to design and test new services.

Interview notes:

MBNQA Standards

Zero-Based — World-Class

| 0 | 10 | 20 | 30 | 40 | 50 | 60 | 70 | 80 | 90 | 100 |

(Circle score that best fits your organization.)

Zero-Based Organization

- No system is in place to ensure consistent design and testing of health care services before releasing to patients and other stakeholders.

- No refined, documented research approach in all areas to ensure consistent quality in design plans and testing before introduction of new services.

World-Class Organization

- All new patient health services are designed and piloted by cross-functional teams.

- Documented health care service procedures are in place to test new services before widespread delivery.

☑ Approach   ☑ Deployment   ☐ Results

Examples of Related JCAHO Compliance

New processes are designed based on the needs and expectations of patients, staff, and others, and up-to-date sources of information about designing processes and the performance of the processes and their outcomes in other organizations are used.

5.1b   Design and testing of new services.

+ Strengths

1.

2.

3.

- Opportunities for Improvement

1.

2.

3.

Strategic Planning Issues:

　　Short Term (1 to 3 years)

　　　1.

　　　2.

　　Long Term (3 years or more)

　　　1.

　　　2.

5.1c   How does your organization systematically evaluate and improve design processes for new service initiation?

Interview notes:

                                  MBNQA
Zero-Based   **Standards**   World-Class

| 0 | 10 | 20 | 30 | 40 | 50 | 60 | 70 | 80 | 90 | 100 |

(Circle score that best fits your organization.)

Zero-Based Organization

- Service design and design processes are not evaluated for improvement.

- New service design is evaluated, but no changes are incorporated into improvement as a result of the evaluation.

World-Class Organization

- Pilots are used for cycle time reduction.

- Program evaluations are conducted by both designers and users during and after new service initiation.

☑ Approach   ☑ Deployment   ☐ Results

Examples of Related JCAHO Compliance

Design or improvement activities specifically consider the expected impact of the design or improvement on the relevant dimensions of performance, set performance expectations, including adopting, adapting or creating measures of performance.

Process Management   119

5.1c   Evaluation and improvement of design processes for new services.

+ Strengths

1.

2.

3.

- Opportunities for Improvement

1.

2.

3.

Strategic Planning Issues:

　　Short Term (1 to 3 years)

　　　1.

　　　2.

　　Long Term (3 years or more)

　　　1.

　　　2.

5.2 NOTES

5.2 Delivery of Patient Health Care (35 points)

Describe how the organization's key patient health care services are managed to ensure design requirements are met and that quality, effectiveness, and efficiency are continuously improved.

AREAS TO ADDRESS

a. how the organization manages key patient health care services to ensure they meet the design requirements addressed in Item 5.1. Describe: (1) the key patient health care services and their principal process requirements; (2) how assessments, measurements, and/or observations are coordinated and used to maintain high performance. Include how the organization ensures that the results are available to appropriate staff.

b. how patients' expectations are addressed and considered in the delivery of services. Describe: (1) how health care service delivery is explained to set realistic patient expectations; (2) how likely health care outcomes are explained to establish realistic patient expectations; and (3) how patient decision-making and preferences are factored into the delivery of health care services.

c. how patient health care services are evaluated and improved to achieve enhanced quality, effectiveness, and efficiency. Describe how each of the following is used or considered: (1) legally mandated assessments and accreditation results; (2) information from patients and their families; (3) benchmarking and research results; (4) use of new and/or alternative technology; and (5) information from other stakeholders concerned with the delivery of patient health care services.

5.2 MBNQA Average Percent Score

[✓] Approach   [✓] Deployment   [ ] Results

5.2a How does your organization ensure that health care service design requirements are met?

Interview notes:

MBNQA
Zero-Based   **Standards**   World-Class

| 0 | 10 | 20 | 30 | 40 | 50 | 60 | 70 | 80 | 90 | 100 |

(Circle score that best fits your organization.)

Zero-Based Organization

- No indicators are in place to gauge out-of-control designs of health care services.

- No quality control processes are in place to ensure that service design requirements are being met.

World-Class Organization

- Staff focus groups are in place to ensure that new patient health care services design meets design requirements.

- Service design is based on patient and other stakeholder requirements.

[✓] Approach   [✓] Deployment   [ ] Results

Examples of Related JCAHO Compliance

The scope of services provided by each department is defined in writing and is approved by the organization's administration, medical staff, or both, as appropriate; all staff-assigned-managerial-responsibilities participate in cross-organizational activities to improve organizational performance, as appropriate to their responsibilities; the leaders adopt an approach to performance improvement that includes at least the following: planning, setting priorities, assessing, implementing, and maintaining improvements.

5.2a   Health care service design requirements are met.

+ Strengths

1.

2.

3.

- Opportunities for Improvement

1.

2.

3.

Strategic Planning Issues:

    Short Term (1 to 3 years)

        1.

        2.

    Long Term (3 years or more)

        1.

        2.

5.2b How does your organization ensure that patient's expectations are addressed and considered in service delivery?

Interview notes:

MBNQA Standards

Zero-Based ———————————————————— World-Class

| 0 | 10 | 20 | 30 | 40 | 50 | 60 | 70 | 80 | 90 | 100 |

(Circle score that best fits your organization.)

Zero-Based Organization

- *Organization is not concerned with addressing patients and other stakeholders expectations regarding services.*

- *Patient expectations regarding service delivery are not considered or reviewed for continuous improvement.*

World-Class Organization

- *Patients and other stakeholders are surveyed to help determine their satisfaction with service delivery.*

- *Cross-functional employee teams are formed to periodically review and assess whether patients' expectations are being addressed in service quality.*

[✓] Approach   [✓] Deployment   [ ] Results

Examples of Related JCAHO Compliance

The organization has a mechanism to respect patients' rights to treatment or service subject to the hospital's capability, mission and applicable law and regulation; this mechanism addresses the patient's involvement in all aspects of care, including obtaining informed consent, resolutions of conflict-of-care decisions, and decisions relative to care at the end of life; the organization collects data about the needs and expectations of patients and others and the degree to which these needs and expectations have been met.

5.2b   Patient's expectations addressed in service delivery.

+ Strengths

1.

2.

3.

- Opportunities for Improvement

1.

2.

3.

Strategic Planning Issues:

    Short Term (1 to 3 years)

        1.

        2.

    Long Term (3 years or more)

        1.

        2.

5.2c How does your organization evaluate and improve the quality, effectiveness, and efficiency of patient health care services?

Interview notes:

MBNQA Standards

Zero-Based　　　　　　　　　　　　　　　　　　　　　　　　World-Class

| 0 | 10 | 20 | 30 | 40 | 50 | 60 | 70 | 80 | 90 | 100 |

(Circle score that best fits your organization.)

Zero-Based Organization

- *No integrated process in place to evaluate and improve the quality, effectiveness, and efficiency of patient care services.*

- *No evidence that organization evaluates the quality, effectiveness, and efficiency of patient care services on a consistent basis.*

World-Class Organization

- *Employees at all levels form teams to review the quality, effectiveness, and efficiency of patient care services.*

- *Rigorous and systematic processes are in place for sampling output and ensuring adherence to design plans.*

☑ Approach　　☑ Deployment　　☐ Results

Examples of Related JCAHO Compliance

The organization gathers, assesses, and takes appropriate action on information that relates to the patient's satisfaction with the services provided; the assessment process includes comparing data about the organization's processes and outcomes over time, comparing the organization's processes to information from up-to-date sources about the design and performance of processes (such as practice guidelines or parameters), and comparing the organization's performance of processes and their outcomes to that of other organizations, including using reference databases; the chief executive officer takes all reasonable steps to provide for organizational compliance with applicable law and regulation, and consistent with governing body policy, the review of and prompt action on reports and recommendations from authorized planning, regulatory, and inspecting agencies.

5.2c   Evaluation and improvement of patient health care services.

+ Strengths

1.

2.

3.

- Opportunities for Improvement

1.

2.

3.

Strategic Planning Issues:

    Short Term (1 to 3 years)

        1.

        2.

    Long Term (3 years or more)

        1.

        2.

5.3 NOTES

5.3 Patient Care Support Services Design and Development (20 points)

Describe how the organization's key patient care support services are designed and managed to meet the organization's requirements for delivery of patient health care services and to drive continuous improvement.

AREAS TO ADDRESS

a. how key patient care support services are designed. Include: (1) how key requirements are determined, taking into account patient and clinical needs; (2) how these requirements are translated into effective and efficient processes, including appropriate measurement plans; and (3) how all delivery requirements are addressed early in design by all appropriate organizational units/departments and suppliers to ensure integration, coordination, and capability.

b. how the organization manages key patient care support services to ensure they meet design requirements. Describe: (1) the key services and their principal process requirements; and (2) how assessments, measurements and/or observations are coordinated and used to maintain high performance.

c. how patient care support services are evaluated and improved to achieve enhanced quality, effectiveness, and efficiency. Describe how each of the following is used or considered: (1) information from patients and their families; (2) benchmarking, assessment, and research results; (3) use of new and/or alternative technology; and (4) information from other stakeholders concerned with the delivery of patient care services.

5.3 MBNQA Average Percent Score

☑ Approach   ☑ Deployment   ☐ Results

5.3a How does your organization determine requirements and design key patient care support services? (e.g., housekeeping services, paging services, medical records and transcription services, laboratory or radiology results services.)

Interview notes:

MBNQA Standards

Zero-Based | | | | | | | | | | | World-Class
| 0 | 10 | 20 | 30 | 40 | 50 | 60 | 70 | 80 | 90 | 100 |

(Circle score that best fits your organization.)

Zero-Based Organization

- Support services are not integrated and coordinated with patient care services.

- No determination and limited consideration is made by the organization to integrate and coordinate support services when designing new patient services.

World-Class Organization

- Patients and other stakeholders are surveyed after discharge to gauge if support services enhance key patient care services.

- Support services are included in the design process of all key patient care services.

☑ Approach   ☑ Deployment   ☐ Results

Examples of Related JCAHO Compliance

The scope of services provided by each department is defined in writing and is approved by the organization's administration, medical staff, or both as appropriate; the leaders adopt an approach to performance improvement that includes at least the following: planning, setting priorities, assessing, implementing, and maintaining improvement.

5.3a   Determination and design of key patient care support services.

+ Strengths

1.

2.

3.

- Opportunities for Improvement

1.

2.

3.

Strategic Planning Issues:

   Short Term (1 to 3 years)

   1.

   2.

   Long Term (3 years or more)

   1.

   2.

5.3b How does the organization ensure that key patient care support services meet design requirements?

Interview notes:

MBNQA
Zero-Based **Standards** World-Class

| 0 | 10 | 20 | 30 | 40 | 50 | 60 | 70 | 80 | 90 | 100 |

(Circle score that best fits your organization.)

Zero-Based Organization

- *No evidence that organization evaluates its support services to ensure that design requirements are met.*

- *Organization does not employ a systematic approach to evaluate and ensure that patient care support services meet design requirements.*

World-Class Organization

- *Organization uses a structured evaluation process to ensure that patient services and support services are coordinated and meet design requirements.*

- *Organization incorporates simple flow charting of its patient support services to ensure better integration with patient health care services.*

☑ Approach ☑ Deployment ☐ Results

Examples of Related JCAHO Compliance

The organization has a planned, systematic, organizationwide approach to designing, measuring, assessing, and improving its performance; the organization has a systematic process in place to collect data needed to (1) design new processes, (2) evaluate performance relative to functions, processes, and outcomes, (3) measure the performance and stability of existing processes, (4) identify improvement opportunities, and (5) assess the effect of changes to processes.

5.3b   Key patient care support services meet design requirements.

+ Strengths

1.

2.

3.

- Opportunities for Improvement

1.

2.

3.

Strategic Planning Issues:

    Short Term (1 to 3 years)

        1.

        2.

    Long Term (3 years or more)

        1.

        2.

134 THE BALDRIGE WORKBOOK FOR HEALTHCARE

5.3c How does your organization assess and improve the quality, effectiveness, and efficiency of patient care services?

Interview notes:

MBNQA Standards

Zero-Based — World-Class

| 0 | 10 | 20 | 30 | 40 | 50 | 60 | 70 | 80 | 90 | 100 |

(Circle score that best fits your organization.)

Zero-Based Organization

- *Organization does not evaluate support services.*

- *Organization inconsistently monitors the quality, effectiveness, and efficiency of patient care support services.*

World-Class Organization

- *Organization conducts benchmarks on a regular basis to identify improvement opportunities within support services.*

- *Organization improves support services based on patient and other stakeholder survey results.*

☑ Approach   ☑ Deployment   ☐ Results

Examples of Related JCAHO Compliance

The organization gathers, assesses, and takes appropriate action on information that relates to the patient's satisfaction with the services provided; the assessment process includes comparing data about the organization's processes and outcomes over time, comparing the organization's processes to information from up-to-date sources about the design and performance of processes (such as practice guidelines or parameters), and comparing the organization's performance of processes and their outcomes to that of other organizations; including using reference databases; the chief executive officer taxes all reasonable steps to provide the organizational compliance with applicable law and regulation, and consistent with governing body policy, the review of and prompt action on reports and recommendations from authorized planning, regulatory, and inspecting agencies; existing processes are improved when an organization decides to act on an opportunity for improvement or when the measurement of an existing processes identifies that an undesirable change in performance may have occurred or is occurring.

5.3c   Organization's assessment and improvement of patient care support services.

+ Strengths

1.

2.

3.

- Opportunities for Improvement

1.

2.

3.

Strategic Planning Issues:

   Short Term (1 to 3 years)

   1.

   2.

   Long Term (3 years or more)

   1.

   2.

5.4 NOTES

5.4 Community Health Services Design and Delivery (15 points)

Describe how key community health services are selected, designed, and managed to support the needs of the community.

AREAS TO ADDRESS

a. how key community health services are selected and designed. Include: (1) how key community health needs are determined; (2) how these needs are translated into effective and efficient processes, including appropriate measurement plans; and (3) how all delivery requirements are addressed early in design by all organizational units/departments and with partners, as appropriate, to ensure integration, coordination, and capability.

b. how the organization manages its key community health services to ensure they meet design requirements. Describe: (1) the key services and their principal process requirements; and (2) how assessments, measurements, and/or observations are used to maintain high performance.

c. how community health services are evaluated, improved, and/or changed to achieve enhanced quality, effectiveness, and efficiency. Describe how each of the following is used or considered: (1) information from the community, including its public and business leaders; (2) community health data; (3) benchmarking and research results; and (4) availability of new and/or alternative technology.

5.4 MBNQA Average Percent Score

☑ Approach   ☑ Deployment   ☐ Results

5.4a How does your organization select and design its key community health services?

Interview notes:

<table>
<tr><td>Zero-Based</td><td colspan="3" align="center">**MBNQA Standards**</td><td>World-Class</td></tr>
<tr><td colspan="5">0　10　20　30　40　50　60　70　80　90　100</td></tr>
</table>

(Circle score that best fits your organization.)

Zero-Based Organization	World-Class Organization
• Organization does not select and design its key community health services.	• Community health services survey data are used to select key health services.
• Key community health services are selected by senior leadership with no input from stakeholders.	• Senior staff ensures that the selection and design of key community health services are integrated with other key initiatives throughout the organization.

☑ Approach   ☑ Deployment   ☐ Results

Examples of Related JCAHO Compliance

Community leaders are involved in planning services; the emergency management plan should include defining and, when appropriate, integrating the organization's role with communitywide emergency preparedness efforts; there should be a high correlation between the content of the mission statement, which should describe the organization's purpose and role in the community, and the content of the organization's plans, budgets, resource allocation, and policies; the leaders individually and jointly develop and participate in systematic and effective mechanisms designed for fostering communication among individuals and components of the organization and coordinating internal activities.

5.4a   Organization's selection and design of key community health services.

+ Strengths

1.

2.

3.

- Opportunities for Improvement

1.

2.

3.

Strategic Planning Issues:

    Short Term (1 to 3 years)

    1.

    2.

    Long Term (3 years or more)

    1.

    2.

5.4b How does your organization ensure that key community health services meet design requirements?

Interview notes:

MBNQA Standards

Zero-Based ———————————————————————— World-Class

| 0 | 10 | 20 | 30 | 40 | 50 | 60 | 70 | 80 | 90 | 100 |

(Circle score that best fits your organization.)

Zero-Based Organization

- Organization has no processes in place to gauge the extent to which key community health services meet design requirements.

- Organization is not concerned that key community health services meet design requirements.

World-Class Organization

- Organization conducts annual assessments of all community health programs to ensure that programs are meeting design requirements.

- Cycle time is measured quarterly within each community health program to maintain high performance standards. Each program has cycle time goals documented.

[✓] Approach   [✓] Deployment   [ ] Results

Examples of Related JCAHO Compliance

The organization has in place a systematic process to collect data needed to (1) design and assess new processes, (2) assess performance relevant to functions, process, and outcome, (3) measure the level of performance and stability of existing processes, (4) identify areas for possible improvement of existing processes, and (5) determine whether changes in the process resulted in improvement.

5.4b   Organization's key community health services meet design requirements.

+ Strengths

1.

2.

3.

- Opportunities for Improvement

1.

2.

3.

Strategic Planning Issues:

　　Short Term (1 to 3 years)

　　　1.

　　　2.

　　Long Term (3 years or more)

　　　1.

　　　2.

5.4c How does your organization evaluate and improve key community health services?

Interview notes:

MBNQA
Zero-Based **Standards** World-Class

| 0 | 10 | 20 | 30 | 40 | 50 | 60 | 70 | 80 | 90 | 100 |

(Circle score that best fits your organization.)

Zero-Based Organization

- *No comparisons or benchmarks are being made of other health care organizations' community health services.*

- *Organization is not concerned with evaluating and improving key community health services.*

World-Class Organization

- *Organization evaluates key community health services by benchmarking other organizations that have been identified as being best within this area.*

- *Measurement indicators have been developed to gauge the benefit that key community health services have on the general health of the public.*

☑ Approach   ☑ Deployment   ☐ Results

Examples of Related JCAHO Compliance

The assessment process includes comparing data about the organization's processes and outcomes over time, comparing the organization's processes to information from up-to-date sources about the design and performance of processes (such as practice guidelines or parameters), and comparing the organization's performance of processes and their outcomes to that of other organizations.

5.4c   Evaluation and improvement of key community health services.

+ Strengths

1.

2.

3.

- Opportunities for Improvement

1.

2.

3.

Strategic Planning Issues:

    Short Term (1 to 3 years)

        1.

        2.

    Long Term (3 years or more)

        1.

        2.

5.5 NOTES

5.5 Administrative and Business Operations Management (20 points)

Describe how the organization's key administrative and business operations are managed so that current requirements are met, health care services are well supported, and operational performance is continuously improved.

AREAS TO ADDRESS

a. how the organization designs and manages key administrative and business operations. Describe: (1) the key operations, their principal customers, and principal requirements; (2) how the principal requirements are translated into effective and efficient processes, including appropriate measurement plans; (3) how these services are designed and managed to support health care delivery by the organization; and (4) how measurements and/or observations are used to maintain high performance.

b. how administrative and business operations are evaluated and improved to achieve better operational performance, including cycle time. Describe how each of the following is used or considered: (1) process analysis and research; (2) benchmarking; and (3) information from customers of the operations—within and outside the organization.

5.5 MBNQA Average Percent Score

☑ Approach   ☑ Deployment   ☐ Results

5.5a How does your organization design and manage key administrative and business operations? (e.g., finance and accounting, information services, plant and facilities management, materials management, marketing, risk management, secretarial and other administrative services.)

Interview notes:

	MBNQA	
Zero-Based	**Standards**	World-Class

| 0 | 10 | 20 | 30 | 40 | 50 | 60 | 70 | 80 | 90 | 100 |

(Circle score that best fits your organization.)

Zero-Based Organization

- *Employee input is not encouraged within administrative and business operations management.*

- *Patient and other stakeholder feedback is not used for process improvement within administrative and business operations.*

World-Class Organization

- *Employee teams identify and flowchart all key processes within administrative and business operations to ensure improved operational performance and cycle time.*

- *Self-directed work teams are deployed within administrative and business operations management to improve work processes.*

[✓] Approach   [✓] Deployment   [ ] Results

Examples of Related JCAHO Compliance

The organization's leaders set expectations, develop plans, and manage processes to assess, improve and maintain the quality of the organization's governance, management, clinical, and support activities; an annual audit of the organization's finances is conducted by an independent public accountant, unless otherwise provided by law;, the chief executive officer, through management and administrative staff, provides for (1)the implementation of organized management and administrative functions throughout the organization, including the establishment of clear lines of responsibility and accountability within departments and between department heads and administrative staff and (2) establishment of internal controls to safeguard physical, financial, information, and human resources.

5.5a   Organization's design and management of key administrative and business operations.

+ Strengths

1.

2.

3.

- Opportunities for Improvement

1.

2.

3.

Strategic Planning Issues:

   Short Term (1 to 3 years)

   1.

   2.

   Long Term (3 years or more)

   1.

   2.

5.5b How does your organization evaluate and improve key administrative and business operations?

Interview notes:

MBNQA
Zero-Based — **Standards** — World-Class

| 0 | 10 | 20 | 30 | 40 | 50 | 60 | 70 | 80 | 90 | 100 |

(Circle score that best fits your organization.)

Zero-Based Organization

- *No patient/stakeholder surveys are conducted to evaluate and improve key administrative and business operations.*

- *Organization does not consistently evaluate its administrative and business operations for improved performance.*

World-Class Organization

- *Patient and stakeholder surveys are conducted within each of the administrative and business operations annually.*

- *Key process benchmarks are identified within administrative and business operations and used to gauge improvement.*

[✓] Approach   [✓] Deployment   [ ] Results

Examples of Related JCAHO Compliance

The organization has a planned, organizationwide approach to designing, measuring, assessing, and improving its performance; all appropriate departments are involved in the design, measurement, assessment, and improvement activities; the organization collects data about the needs and expectations of patients and others and the degree to which these needs and expectations have been met; the assessment includes comparing data about the organization's processes and outcomes over time, comparing the organization's processes to information from up-to-date sources about the design and performance of processes (such as practice guideline of parameters), and comparing the organization's performance of processes and their outcomes to that of other organizations, including using reference databases.

5.5b   Evaluation and improvement of key administrative and business operations.

+ Strengths

1.

2.

3.

- Opportunities for Improvement

1.

2.

3.

Strategic Planning Issues:

   Short Term (1 to 3 years)

   1.

   2.

   Long Term (3 years or more)

   1.

   2.

5.6 NOTES

5.6 Community Health Services Design and Delivery (15 points)

Describe how the organization assures that materials, instrumentation and devices, and services furnished by others meet the organization's requirements. Describe also the organization's actions and plans to improve supplier relationships.

AREAS TO ADDRESS

a. summary of the organization's key requirements and how they are communicated to suppliers. Include: (1) a brief summary of the principal requirements for key suppliers, the measures and/or indicators associated with these requirements, and the expected performance levels; (2) how the organization determines whether or not its requirements are met by suppliers; and (3) how performance information is fed back to suppliers.

b. how the organization evaluates and improves its supplier relationships. Describe current actions and plans: (1) to improve suppliers' abilities to meet requirements; and (2) to improve procurement processes, including feedback sought from suppliers.

5.6 MBNQA Average Percent Score

☑ Approach   ☑ Deployment   ☐ Results

5.6a How does your organization communicate key requirements to outside providers of goods and services?

Interview notes:

$$\text{Zero-Based} \quad\quad\quad \textbf{MBNQA Standards} \quad\quad\quad \text{World-Class}$$

| 0 | 10 | 20 | 30 | 40 | 50 | 60 | 70 | 80 | 90 | 100 |

(Circle score that best fits your organization.)

Zero-Based Organization

- No system is in place for supplier partnership or supplier certification.

- Organization does not consider supplier performance to be a major hindrance and does not define its requirements to suppliers.

World-Class Organization

- Organization has a formal supplier certification process in place.

- Organization has published quarterly requirements for all critical suppliers.

☑ Approach ☑ Deployment ☐ Results

Examples of Related JCAHO Compliance

The medical staff has a mechanism used to review credentials and to delineate individual clinical privileges. The organization establishes hospital-specific mechanisms for appointing and reappointing medical staff members and for granting and renewing or revising clinical privileges.

5.6a   Communication of requirements to suppliers.

+ Strengths

1.

2.

3.

- Opportunities for Improvement

1.

2.

3.

Strategic Planning Issues:

    Short Term (1 to 3 years)

        1.

        2.

    Long Term (3 years or more)

        1.

        2.

5.6b Does your organization evaluate and improve its supplier relationships?

Interview notes:

	MBNQA	
Zero-Based	**Standards**	World-Class

| 0 | 10 | 20 | 30 | 40 | 50 | 60 | 70 | 80 | 90 | 100 |

(Circle score that best fits your organization.)

Zero-Based Organization

- Organization considers its suppliers to be the best and does no evaluation.

- Organization does not consider suppliers as partners in its quality improvement initiatives.

World-Class Organization

- Organization has developed a supplier report card system for key suppliers and reviews results monthly.

- Productivity and waste reduction among key suppliers are reviewed by employee-supplier teams each quarter.

☑ Approach   ☑ Deployment   ☐ Results

Examples of Related JCAHO Compliance

Mechanisms for medical staff appointment and reappointment are fully described in the bylaws, rules and regulations, and policies of the medical staff and hospital.

5.6b   Evaluation and improvement of supplier relationships.

+ Strengths

1.

2.

3.

- Opportunities for Improvement

1.

2.

3.

Strategic Planning Issues:

    Short Term (1 to 3 years)

        1.

        2.

    Long Term (3 years or more)

        1.

        2.

CHAPTER EIGHT

Category 6.0 Organizational Performance Results

6.0 Organizational Performance Results (250 points)

The *Organizational Performance Results* Category examines performance and improvement in key patient health care areas, in patient care support service quality, and in community health services. Performance and improvement are assessed in administrative/business areas—productivity and operational effectiveness, supplier performance, and financial performance indicators linked to these areas. Also examined are performance levels relative to competitors and other institutions providing similar health care services.

6.1 NOTES

Organizational Performance Results 159

6.1 Patient Health Care Results (80 points)

Summarize current trends and results of improvement efforts for key measures and/or indicators of patient health.

AREAS TO ADDRESS

a. for major health care services provided, give current levels and trends in key measures and/or indicators of patient health and the improvement of patient health.

b. for the results reported in 6.1a, provide appropriate comparative data for other institutions providing similar health care services.

6.1 MBNQA Average Percent Score

☐ Approach ☐ Deployment ✓ Results

6.1a Does your organization collect current levels and trend data related to quality improvement of patient health?

Interview notes:

	MBNQA	
Zero-Based	**Standards**	World-Class

| 0 | 10 | 20 | 30 | 40 | 50 | 60 | 70 | 80 | 90 | 100 |

(Circle score that best fits your organization.)

Zero-Based Organization

- *Organization only collects data in clinical areas.*

- *Organization collects data but does not consistently use them to improve major health care services and patient health.*

World-Class Organization

- *Trend data are collected by the organization on patient health care service quality.*

- *Organization collects data and trends on nosocomial infections, length of stay, hospital readmissions, and clinical outcomes.*

☐ Approach   ☐ Deployment   ☑ Results

Examples of Related JCAHO Compliance

The collected data includes both processes and outcomes; the post-procedure period is monitored including (1) the patient's psychological and mental status, (2) pathological findings (when indicated), (3) any unusual or postoperative complications and the management of those events and complications, and (4) if appropriate, the patient's impairments and functional status; an objective of the nosocomial infection risk reduction process is improvement in the risks of, trends in, and where appropriate, rates of epidemiologically significant infections.

Organizational Performance Results   161

6.1a   Collection of levels and trend data for quality improvement of patient health.

+ Strengths

1.

2.

3.

- Opportunities for Improvement

1.

2.

3.

Strategic Planning Issues:

　　Short Term (1 to 3 years)

　　　1.

　　　2.

　　Long Term (3 years or more)

　　　1.

　　　2.

6.1b Specifically, how does your organization compare its quality results against providers of similar health care services?

Interview notes:

	MBNQA	
Zero-Based	**Standards**	World-Class

| 0 | 10 | 20 | 30 | 40 | 50 | 60 | 70 | 80 | 90 | 100 |

(Circle score that best fits your organization.)

Zero-Based Organization

- *No formal benchmarking process is conducted within the organization.*

- *Comparison data used for process improvements appear anecdotal rather than being based on factual comparison or benchmark data.*

World-Class Organization

- *Organization conducts benchmarks against other health care organizations to compare quality results of key processes that are known for "best practices."*

- *Organization has prioritized and selected five key processes that are used for comparison against other health care providers identified as having "best practices" within these identified processes.*

☐ Approach ☐ Deployment ☑ Results

Examples of Related JCAHO Compliance

The assessment process includes comparing data about the organization's processes and outcomes over time, comparing the organization's performance of processes and their outcomes to that of other organizations, including using reference databases.

6.1b   Organization's quality level comparisons against similar health care providers.

+ Strengths

1.

2.

3.

- Opportunities for Improvement

1.

2.

3.

Strategic Planning Issues:

    Short Term (1 to 3 years)

        1.

        2.

    Long Term (3 years or more)

        1.

        2.

6.2 NOTES

6.2 Patient Care Support Services Results (40 points)

Summarize current trends and results of improvement efforts for key measure and/or indicators of patient care support service quality.

AREAS TO ADDRESS

a. for major patient care support services, give current levels and trends in key measures and/or indicators of patient support service quality. Graphs and tables should include appropriate comparative data.

6.2 MBNQA Average Percent Score

☐ Approach   ☐ Deployment   ☑ Results

6.2a Does your organization collect current levels and trend data related to quality improvement of major patient care support services?

Interview notes:

MBNQA
Zero-Based **Standards** World-Class

| 0 | 10 | 20 | 30 | 40 | 50 | 60 | 70 | 80 | 90 | 100 |

(Circle score that best fits your organization.)

Zero-Based Organization

- *No trend data on service quality are in place within patient care support services.*

- *Data collected from key patient care support services are not trended or used to support quality improvement.*

World-Class Organization

- *Housekeeping and medical records data are collected and charted on graphs.*

- *Pharmacy collects cycle time data on prescriptions and completes a trend analysis on the results each quarter.*

☐ Approach ☐ Deployment ☑ Results

Examples of Related JCAHO Compliance

The collected data includes both processes and outcomes; the post-procedure period is monitored including (1) the patient's psychological and mental status, (2) pathological findings (when indicated), (3) any unusual or postoperative complications and the management of those events and complications, and (4) if appropriate, the patient's impairments and functional status; an objective of the nosocomial infection risk reduction process is improvement in the risks of, trends in, and where appropriate, rates of epidemiologically significant infections.

6.2a Organization's collection of current levels and trend data for quality improvement of major patient care support services.

+ Strengths

1.

2.

3.

- Opportunities for Improvement

1.

2.

3.

Strategic Planning Issues:

   Short Term (1 to 3 years)

   1.

   2.

   Long Term (3 years or more)

   1.

   2.

6.3 NOTES

6.3 Community Health Services Results (30 points)

Summarize current trends and results of improvement efforts using key measures and/or indicators of the organization's contributions to community health.

> **AREAS TO ADDRESS**
>
> **a.** current levels and trends in key measures and/or indicators of the organization's contributions to community health and of the impact of these contributions on improving community health. Graphs and tables should include appropriate data.

6.3 MBNQA Average Percent Score

☐ Approach ☐ Deployment ☑ Results

6.3a Does your organization collect data on the impact that its health care activities have on improving community health?

Interview notes:

MBNQA Standards

Zero-Based World-Class

| 0 | 10 | 20 | 30 | 40 | 50 | 60 | 70 | 80 | 90 | 100 |

(Circle score that best fits your organization.)

<u>Zero-Based Organization</u>

- *Organization does not collect data on its community health care activities.*

- *Community health service data on the organization's educational programs, immunization programs, hypertension and cholesterol screening are not collected.*

<u>World-Class Organization</u>

- *Organization collects data on all community health care initiatives in which it is involved.*

- *Organization collects data on community health fairs and measures the impact these initiatives have on community health.*

☐ Approach ☐ Deployment ☑ Results

Examples of Related JCAHO Compliance

The organization's leaders and, as appropriate, community leaders and other organizations collaborate to design services. Services are designed to be responsive to the needs and expectation of patients and/or families/decision makers.

6.3a   Data collected on impact the organization has on improving community health.

+ Strengths

1.

2.

3.

- Opportunities for Improvement

1.

2.

3.

Strategic Planning Issues:

　　Short Term (1 to 3 years)

　　　1.

　　　2.

　　Long Term (3 years or more)

　　　1.

　　　2.

6.4 NOTES

6.4 Administrative, Business, and Supplier Results (90 points)

Summarize results of improvement efforts using key measures and/or indicators of administrative, business, and supplier performance and or financial outcomes.

AREAS TO ADDRESS

a. current levels and trends in key measures and/or indicators of administrative, business, and supplier performance and of financial outcomes. Graphs and tables should include appropriate comparative data.

☐ Approach ☐ Deployment ☑ Results

☐ 6.4 MBNQA Average Percent Score

6.4a How does your organization track improvement of administrative, business, and supplier performance?

Interview notes:

MBNQA Standards

Zero-Based — World-Class

| 0 | 10 | 20 | 30 | 40 | 50 | 60 | 70 | 80 | 90 | 100 |

(Circle score that best fits your organization.)

Zero-Based Organization

- *Quality results of key supplies are not tracked.*

- *The organization tracks clinical areas but conducts limited tracking of administrative, business, and financial performance.*

World-Class Organization

- *Quality audits of suppliers are conducted and improvement results are tracked.*

- *Cost per patient and average operating income per patient are tracked and the results are trended and incorporated into process improvements.*

☐ Approach ☐ Deployment ☑ Results

6.4a   Current levels and trends of administrative, business, and supplier performance.

+ Strengths

1.

2.

3.

- Opportunities for Improvement

1.

2.

3.

Strategic Planning Issues:

   Short Term (1 to 3 years)

     1.

     2.

   Long Term (3 years or more)

     1.

     2.

6.5 NOTES

6.5 Accreditation and Assessment Results (10 points)

Summarize results of accreditation and assessment findings and results of improvement activities using key performance measures and/or indicators.

AREAS TO ADDRESS

a. results in key measures and/or indicators of organizational accreditation and assessment performance. Graphs and tables should include appropriate comparative data.

6.5 MBNQA Average Percent Score

☐ Approach ☐ Deployment ☑ Results

6.5a   How does your organization track accreditation and assessment results?

Interview notes:

MBNQA Standards

Zero-Based — World-Class

| 0 | 10 | 20 | 30 | 40 | 50 | 60 | 70 | 80 | 90 | 100 |

(Circle score that best fits your organization.)

Zero-Based Organization

- *Organization tracks only clinical and regulatory areas and is not concerned with using assessment results for process improvement.*

- *Organization has limited measurement plans in place for patient care support services.*

World-Class Organization

- *Organization tracks JCAHO accreditation findings, regulatory reviews, staff licenser and recredentialling determinations, Baldrige assessment results, proficiency testing results, and utilization review results.*

- *Organization tracks cycle time reduction within key processes, employee training results, safety, waste reduction, and continuing education requirements for professional staff.*

☐ Approach   ☐ Deployment   ☑ Results

Examples of Related JCAHO Compliance

The chief executive officer takes all reasonable steps to provide for organizational compliance with applicable law and regulation, and consistent with governing body policy, the review of and prompt action on reports and recommendations from authorized planning, regulatory, and inspecting agencies.

6.5a   Organization's tracking of accreditation and assessment results.

+ Strengths

1.

2.

3.

- Opportunities for Improvement

1.

2.

3.

Strategic Planning Issues:

    Short Term (1 to 3 years)

        1.

        2.

    Long Term (3 years or more)

        1.

        2.

CHAPTER NINE

Category 7.0 Focus on and Satisfaction of Patients and Other Stakeholders

7.0　Focus on and Satisfaction of Patients and Other Stakeholders　(250 points)

The *Focus on and Satisfaction of Patients and Other Stakeholders* Category examines the organization's systems for learning about its patients and other stakeholders, and for building and maintaining its relationships with patients and other important stakeholders. Also examined are levels and trends in key measures of success in delivering patient care services—patient satisfaction, loyalty, and referrals; satisfaction of other stakeholders, including retention of their business; market share in delivered services; and satisfaction relative to competitors.

7.1 NOTES

7.1 Patient and Health Care Market Knowledge (30 points)

Describe how the organization determines near-term and longer-term requirements and expectations of patients and the health care marketplace, and develops listening and learning strategies to understand and anticipate changing needs and demands.

AREAS TO ADDRESS

a. how the organization determines current and near-term requirements and expectations of patients and other stakeholders. Include: (1) how patient groups and/or health care market segments are determined and/or selected, including how patients of competitors and other potential patients or market segments are considered; (2) how information is collected, including what information is sought, frequency and methods of collection, and how objectivity and validity are ensured; (3) how specific patient care services and the relative importance of these services to patient groups or market segments are determined; (4) how specific service features and the relative importance of these services to other stakeholders are determined; (5) how potentially differing expectations of patients and other stakeholders are addressed/reconciled; and (6) how other key information and data such as complaints, gains and losses of patients and patient groups, and patient care and stakeholder service results are used to support the determination.

b. how the organization addresses future requirements and expectations of patients and other stakeholders. Include: (1) an outline of key listening and learning strategies used; and (2) how potentially differing expectations of patients and other stakeholders are addressed/reconciled.

c. how the organization evaluates and improves its processes for determining patient and stakeholder requirements and expectations.

7.1 MBNQA Average Percent Score

☑ Approach ☑ Deployment ☐ Results

184   THE BALDRIGE WORKBOOK FOR HEALTHCARE

7.1a   How does your organization determine requirements and expectations of current patients and other stakeholders?

Interview notes:

	MBNQA	
Zero-Based	**Standards**	World-Class

| 0 | 10 | 20 | 30 | 40 | 50 | 60 | 70 | 80 | 90 | 100 |

(Circle score that best fits your organization.)

Zero-Based Organization

- *No patient/stakeholder surveys, focus groups, or monitoring of competitive factors are in place.*

- *Patients/stakeholders are not segmented and surveyed regarding their requirements and expectations.*

World-Class Organization

- *Current and near-term requirements and expectations of patients and other stakeholders are determined by surveys, focus groups, and benchmark data.*

- *Organization holds semiannual patient/stakeholder focus groups and surveys to ensure that end-user expectations are being met.*

[✓] Approach   [✓] Deployment   [ ] Results

Examples of Related JCAHO Compliance

The organization's leaders, and, as appropriate, community leaders and organizations, collaborate to design services; the design of patient care services to be provided throughout the organization is appropriate to the scope and level of care required by the patients served; services are designed to be responsive to the needs and expectations of patients and/or their families/decision makers; the organization gathers, assesses, and takes appropriate action on information that relates to the patient's satisfaction with the services provided.

7.1a Organization determines requirements and expectations of current patients and other stakeholders.

+ Strengths

1.

2.

3.

- Opportunities for Improvement

1.

2.

3.

Strategic Planning Issues:

   Short Term (1 to 3 years)

   1.

   2.

   Long Term (3 years or more)

   1.

   2.

7.1b How does your organization determine future patient and stakeholder requirements and expectations?

Interview notes:

MBNQA Standards

Zero-Based   World-Class

| 0 | 10 | 20 | 30 | 40 | 50 | 60 | 70 | 80 | 90 | 100 |

(Circle score that best fits your organization.)

Zero-Based Organization

- *No competitive benchmarking takes place within the organization to determine future patient/stakeholder requirements and expectations.*

- *Organization does not train staff in patient/stakeholder follow-up, relationship strategies, or close monitoring of demographic factors that may have a bearing upon patient/stakeholder requirements and expectations.*

World-Class Organization

- *Cross-functional teams undertake the task of projecting future requirements and expectation of patients/stakeholders through ongoing follow-up.*

- *Patient/stakeholder contact staff meet monthly in focus groups with patients and stakeholders to determine future requirements and expectations.*

[✓] Approach   [✓] Deployment   [ ] Results

Examples of Related JCAHO Compliance

The organization collects data about the needs and expectations of patients and others and the degree to which these needs and expectations have been met.

7.1b   Determination of future patient and stakeholder requirements and expectations.

+ Strengths

1.

2.

3.

- Opportunities for Improvement

1.

2.

3.

Strategic Planning Issues:

    Short Term (1 to 3 years)

    1.

    2.

    Long Term (3 years or more)

    1.

    2.

7.1c How does your organization evaluate and improve its processes for determining patient and stakeholder requirements and expectations?

Interview notes:

MBNQA Standards

Zero-Based │ 0 10 20 30 40 50 60 70 80 90 100 │ World-Class

(Circle score that best fits your organization.)

Zero-Based Organization

- Organization surveys current patients and stakeholders, but does not use this data to meet its requirements and expectations.

- Organization's survey process has not been validated by a third party and survey results are not addressing key patient/stakeholder issues.

World-Class Organization

- Organization uses patient/stakeholder focus groups and advisory councils to address patient/stakeholder requirements and expectations.

- Organization has a survey process in place to determine patient/stakeholder requirements and expectations.

[✓] Approach   [✓] Deployment   [ ] Results

Examples of Related JCAHO Compliance

The organization has a planned, systematic, organizationwide approach to designing, measuring, assessing, and improving its performance; the organization gathers, assesses, and takes appropriate action on information that relates to the patient's satisfaction with the services provided.

7.1c Organization's evaluation of its processes for determining patient and stakeholders' requirements and expectations.

+ Strengths

1.

2.

3.

- Opportunities for Improvement

1.

2.

3.

Strategic Planning Issues:

Short Term (1 to 3 years)

1.

2.

Long Term (3 years or more)

1.

2.

7.2 NOTES

7.2 Patient/Stakeholder Relationship Management (30 points)

Describe how the organization provides effective management of its interactions with patients and other stakeholders to preserve and build relationships and to increase knowledge about patients/stakeholders and their expectations.

AREAS TO ADDRESS

a. how the organization provides information and easy access to enable patients and other stakeholders to seek information and assistance, to comment, and to complain. Describe contact management performance measures and service commitments and how these requirements are set, deployed, and tracked.

b. how the organization ensures that formal and informal complaints and feedback received by all organizational units/departments are resolved effectively and promptly. Briefly describe the complaint management process and how it ensures effective recovery of patient and stakeholder confidence, meeting requirements for resolution effectiveness and elimination of the causes of complaints.

c. how the organization follows up with patients on recently delivered patient care services and on patient care service offerings to resolve problems, to seek feedback for improvement, and to build relationships.

d. how the organization follows up with other stakeholders on services and recent interactions to resolve problems, to seek feedback for improvement, and to build relationships.

e. how the organization evaluates and improves its patient and stakeholder relationship management. Include: (1) how service commitments, including those related to patient and other stakeholder access and complaint management, are improved based on patient/stakeholder information; (2) aggregation and use of patient and stakeholder comments and complaints throughout the organization; and (3) how knowledge about patients and other stakeholders is accumulated and used.

7.2 MBNQA Average Percent Score

☑ Approach   ☑ Deployment   ☐ Results

7.2a How does your organization ensure that patients and stakeholders can seek assistance, comment, and/or complain about services?

Interview notes:

MBNQA Standards

Zero-Based   World-Class

| 0 | 10 | 20 | 30 | 40 | 50 | 60 | 70 | 80 | 90 | 100 |

(Circle score that best fits your organization.)

Zero-Based Organization

- *Organization does not provide easy access for patients/stakeholders seeking information and assistance.*

- *Patient and stakeholder input is not encouraged.*

World-Class Organization

- *Organization has a 24-hour help desk in place to provide easy access for patients/stakeholders seeking information and assistance.*

- *Organization measures percentage of resolutions achieved by initial contact staff, number of transfers, and resolution response time for patients/stakeholders.*

[✓] Approach   [✓] Deployment   [ ] Results

Examples of Related JCAHO Compliance

The organization has mechanisms to (1) obtain informed consent, (2) resolve conflict in care or treatment decisions, (3) provide for resolution of complaints; the patient and/or his/her family are provided with appropriate education and training to expand their knowledge of the patient's illness and treatment needs and to learn skills and behaviors that promote recovery and increase function.

7.2a   Organization provides easy access for patient/stakeholder assistance, comments, and complaints.

+ Strengths

1.

2.

3.

- Opportunities for Improvement

1.

2.

3.

Strategic Planning Issues:

   Short Term (1 to 3 years)

   1.

   2.

   Long Term (3 years or more)

   1.

   2.

7.2b How does your organization ensure that patient's expectations are addressed and considered in service delivery?

Interview notes:

MBNQA Standards

Zero-Based ——————————————————————— World-Class

| 0 | 10 | 20 | 30 | 40 | 50 | 60 | 70 | 80 | 90 | 100 |

(Circle score that best fits your organization.)

Zero-Based Organization

- *Organization does not collect formal and informal complaint data from patients/stakeholders.*

- *Organization does not aggregate complaint data from all sources for evaluation and use the results for process improvements.*

World-Class Organization

- *Organization collects all formal and informal patient/stakeholder complaints and feedback and enters them into a database in its mainframe computer. This data is then distributed to appropriate departments.*

- *Organization uses customer complaint data to improve patient/stakeholder contact training.*

☑ Approach   ☑ Deployment   ☐ Results

Examples of Related JCAHO Compliance

The organization has mechanisms to resolve conflict in care or treatment decisions and to provide for resolution of complaints.

7.2b   Patient's expectations addressed in service delivery.

+ Strengths

1.

2.

3.

- Opportunities for Improvement

1.

2.

3.

Strategic Planning Issues:

　　Short Term (1 to 3 years)

　　　1.

　　　2.

　　Long Term (3 years or more)

　　　1.

　　　2.

7.2c How are patient complaints followed up and incorporated into process improvements?

Interview notes:

	MBNQA	
Zero-Based	**Standards**	World-Class

| 0 | 10 | 20 | 30 | 40 | 50 | 60 | 70 | 80 | 90 | 100 |

(Circle score that best fits your organization.)

Zero-Based Organization

- *No consistent patient complaint follow-up process exists.*

- *Patient follow-up is not considered a priority by the organization.*

World-Class Organization

- *Organization has a documented follow-up process for patients who have complaints.*

- *Priorities for improvement projects are set based on patient complaint data.*

☑ Approach   ☑ Deployment   ☐ Results

Examples of Related JCAHO Compliance

The organization collects data about the needs and expectations of patients and others and the degree to which these needs and expectations have been met; the organization has a mechanism for resolution of complaints.

7.2c   Patient complaint follow-up.

+ Strengths

1.

2.

3.

- Opportunities for Improvement

1.

2.

3.

Strategic Planning Issues:

    Short Term (1 to 3 years)

        1.

        2.

    Long Term (3 years or more)

        1.

        2.

7.2d How are stakeholders services and recent interactions followed up?

Interview notes:

MBNQA Standards

Zero-Based │ 0 10 20 30 40 50 60 70 80 90 100 │ World-Class

(Circle score that best fits your organization.)

Zero-Based Organization

- *Organization does not have consistent follow-up procedures in place.*

- *Organization does not have a process in place to aggregate stakeholder complaint data for service quality improvement.*

World-Class Organization

- *Organization conducts formal exit interviews with all stakeholders who receive services and a formal follow-up procedure is in place.*

- *A letter from senior administrators is sent to all stakeholders who issue complaints or experience service problems.*

☑ Approach   ☑ Deployment   ☐ Results

Examples of Related JCAHO Compliance

The organization collects data about the needs and expectations of patients and others and the degree to which these needs and expectations have been met; the organization has a mechanism for resolution of complaints.

7.2d   Stakeholder follow-up for services and recent interactions.

+ Strengths

1.

2.

3.

- Opportunities for Improvement

1.

2.

3.

Strategic Planning Issues:

Short Term (1 to 3 years)

1.

2.

Long Term (3 years or more)

1.

2.

7.2e How does your organization evaluate and improve its relationship management with patients and stakeholders?

Interview notes:

MBNQA
Zero-Based — **Standards** — World-Class

| 0 | 10 | 20 | 30 | 40 | 50 | 60 | 70 | 80 | 90 | 100 |

(Circle score that best fits your organization.)

Zero-Based Organization

- *No formal process exists for improving patient/stakeholder relationships.*

- *Patient/stakeholder relationship evaluation and training do not exist within the organization.*

World-Class Organization

- *Formal process in place to improve relationships with patients/stakeholders (e.g., patient/stakeholder relationship training, published service standards for patients/stakeholders, etc.)*

- *All patient/stakeholder data are aggregated and used to improve patient/stakeholder relationship management.*

[✓] Approach [✓] Deployment [ ] Results

Examples of Related JCAHO Compliance

The organization collects data about the needs and expectations of patients and others and the degree to which these needs and expectations have been met.

7.2e   Relationship management of patients and stakeholders are evaluated and improved.

+ Strengths

1.

2.

3.

- Opportunities for Improvement

1.

2.

3.

Strategic Planning Issues:

   Short Term (1 to 3 years)

   1.

   2.

   Long Term (3 years or more)

   1.

   2.

7.3 NOTES

7.3 Patient/Stakeholder Satisfaction Determination (30 points)

Describe how the organization determines patient and other stakeholder satisfaction, loyalty, and satisfaction relative to competitors and other organizations delivering similar health care services; describe how these determination processes are evaluated and improved.

AREAS TO ADDRESS

a. how the organization determines patient and other stakeholder satisfaction. Include: (1) a brief description of processes and measurement scales used; frequency of determinations; and how objectivity and validity are ensured. Indicate significant differences in processes and measurement scales for different patient groups, stakeholder groups, and market segments; (2) how patient satisfaction measurements capture key information that reflects patients' likely future health care service delivery decisions, such as provider loyalty and/or positive referrals; and (3) how stakeholder satisfaction measurements capture key information that reflects stakeholders' likely future market behavior, such as repurchase intentions, exclusive provider agreements, and/or positive referrals.

b. how patient and stakeholder satisfaction relative to that for competitors and other organizations delivering similar health care services is determined. Describe: (1) organization-based comparative studies; and (2) comparative studies or evaluations made by independent and/or patient or stakeholder groups. For (1) and (2), describe how the objectivity and validity of studies or evaluation are ensured.

c. how the organization evaluates and improves its overall processes and measurement scales for determining patient and stakeholder satisfaction and satisfaction relative to that for competitors and other organizations delivering similar health care services. Include how other indicators (such as gains and losses of patients or service contracts) and dissatisfaction indicators are used in this improvement process. Describe also how the evaluation takes into account the effectiveness of the use of patient and stakeholder satisfaction information and data throughout the organization.

7.3 MBNQA Average Percent Score

[✓] Approach   [✓] Deployment   [ ] Results

7.3a How does your organization determine patient and stakeholder satisfaction for its different patient/stakeholder groups?

Interview notes:

MBNQA Standards

Zero-Based | 0 10 20 30 40 50 60 70 80 90 100 | World-Class

(Circle score that best fits your organization.)

Zero-Based Organization

- Organization conducts surveys among patient and stakeholder groups but does not aggregate the data and segment markets to determine satisfaction.

- Organization does not recognize differences in patient groups and stakeholder groups.

World-Class Organization

- Organization determines satisfaction for its different patient groups, stakeholder groups, and market segments through annual surveys and focus groups.

- Patient/stakeholder dissatisfaction data are collected and aggregated and used to determine satisfaction.

☑ Approach ☑ Deployment ☐ Results

Examples of Related JCAHO Compliance

The organization collects data about the needs and expectations of patients and others and the degree to which these needs and expectations have been met; the organization has a planned systematic, organizationwide approach to designing, measuring, assessing, and improving its performance.

7.3a   Organization's determination of satisfaction for patient/stakeholder groups.

+ Strengths

1.

2.

3.

- Opportunities for Improvement

1.

2.

3.

Strategic Planning Issues:

   Short Term (1 to 3 years)

   1.

   2.

   Long Term (3 years or more)

   1.

   2.

7.3b How does the organization's patient/stakeholder satisfaction level compare to that of your competitors?

Interview notes:

MBNQA Standards

Zero-Based | World-Class

| 0 | 10 | 20 | 30 | 40 | 50 | 60 | 70 | 80 | 90 | 100 |

(Circle score that best fits your organization.)

Zero-Based Organization

- Organization has no concern for comparing its patient/stakeholder satisfaction against competitors.

- Organization conducts no comparative studies regarding patient/stakeholder satisfaction relative to that of competitors.

World-Class Organization

- Patient/stakeholder surveys and focus groups are used to collect data regarding patient/stakeholder satisfaction relative to that of competitors.

- An independent organization is used to survey patients' and stakeholders' satisfaction with the organization and their comparative satisfaction with competitive organizations.

☑ Approach ☑ Deployment ☐ Results

7.3b   Organization's determination of patient/stakeholder satisfaction relative to competitors.

+ Strengths

1.

2.

3.

- Opportunities for Improvement

1.

2.

3.

Strategic Planning Issues:

   Short Term (1 to 3 years)

   1.

   2.

   Long Term (3 years or more)

   1.

   2.

7.3c How does your organization evaluate and improve its overall processes and measurement scales for determining patient/stakeholder satisfaction relative to that of competitors?

Interview notes:

MBNQA Standards

Zero-Based   World-Class

| 0 | 10 | 20 | 30 | 40 | 50 | 60 | 70 | 80 | 90 | 100 |

(Circle score that best fits your organization.)

Zero-Based Organization

- Organization does not validate measurement indicators used to determine patient/stakeholder satisfaction and then satisfaction relative to that of competitors and other organizations delivering similar health care services.

- Organization does not link patient/stakeholder survey responses to key health care services and cost revenue implications and thus provide a useful basis for improvement.

World-Class Organization

- Organization involves patient/stakeholder contact employees and benchmark data in determining patient/stakeholder satisfaction relative to that of competitors.

- Measurement indicators used for determining patient/stakeholder satisfaction and satisfaction relative to that of competitors are validated by a third party.

[✓] Approach   [✓] Deployment   [ ] Results

Examples of Related JCAHO Compliance

Existing processes are improved when an organization decides to act on an opportunity for improvement or when the measurement of an existing process identifies that an undesirable change may have occurred or is occurring.

7.3c Evaluation and improvement of overall processes and measurement scales for determining patient/stakeholder satisfaction relative to that of competitors.

+ Strengths

1.

2.

3.

- Opportunities for Improvement

1.

2.

3.

Strategic Planning Issues:

    Short Term (1 to 3 years)

        1.

        2.

    Long Term (3 years or more)

        1.

        2.

7.4 NOTES

7.4 Patient/Stakeholder Satisfaction Results (100 points)

Summarize the organization's patient and other stakeholder satisfaction and dissatisfaction results using key measures and/or indicators of these results.

AREAS TO ADDRESS

a. current levels and trends in key measures and/or indicators of: (1) patient satisfaction and patient loyalty; and (2) patient dissatisfaction. Results should be segmented by patient group, as appropriate.

b. current levels and trends in key measures and/or indicators of: (1) other stakeholder satisfaction and loyalty to the organization; and (2) other stakeholder dissatisfaction. Results should be segmented by stakeholder group, as appropriate.

7.4 MBNQA Average Percent Score

☐ Approach   ☐ Deployment   ☑ Results

7.4a Do you collect and segment trend data that measures patient satisfaction and dissatisfaction?

Interview notes:

MBNQA Standards

Zero-Based   World-Class

| 0 | 10 | 20 | 30 | 40 | 50 | 60 | 70 | 80 | 90 | 100 |

(Circle score that best fits your organization.)

Zero-Based Organization

- *Organization does not use survey trend data to determine patient satisfaction and loyalty.*

- *Patient dissatisfaction data are not trended or used for service improvement within the organization.*

World-Class Organization

- *Organization collects trend data to measure current and past patient satisfaction.*

- *Dissatisfaction trend data are aggregated and used to improve patient services throughout the organization.*

☐ Approach   ☐ Deployment   ☑ Results

Examples of Related JCAHO Compliance

The organization collects data about the needs and expectations of patients and others and the degree to which these needs and expectations have been met.

7.4a   Trend data on patient satisfaction and dissatisfaction.

+ Strengths

1.

2.

3.

- Opportunities for Improvement

1.

2.

3.

Strategic Planning Issues:

    Short Term (1 to 3 years)

        1.

        2.

    Long Term (3 years or more)

        1.

        2.

7.4b Do you collect and segment trend data that measures stakeholder satisfaction and dissatisfaction?

Interview notes:

MBNQA Standards

Zero-Based | | | | | | | | | | World-Class
| 0 | 10 | 20 | 30 | 40 | 50 | 60 | 70 | 80 | 90 | 100 |

(Circle score that best fits your organization.)

Zero-Based Organization

- *Key stakeholder dissatisfaction is not addressed.*

- *Stakeholder dissatisfaction data are collected and aggregated, but not incorporated into the organization's planning process.*

World-Class Organization

- *Stakeholders are surveyed quarterly regarding their satisfaction with long-term health care outcomes. The data are trended and incorporated into the organization's annual planning process.*

- *Organization leads other competitive health care providers in reducing adverse stakeholder indicators. Results are segmented by stakeholder group.*

☐ Approach ☐ Deployment ☑ Results

Examples of Related JCAHO Compliance

The organization collects data about the needs and expectations of patients and others and the degree to which these needs and expectations have been met.

7.4b   Trend data on stakeholder satisfaction and dissatisfaction.

+ Strengths

1.

2.

3.

- Opportunities for Improvement

1.

2.

3.

Strategic Planning Issues:

    Short Term (1 to 3 years)

    1.

    2.

    Long Term (3 years or more)

    1.

    2.

7.5 NOTES

7.5 Patient/Stakeholder Satisfaction Comparison (60 points)

Compare the organization's patient and other stakeholder satisfaction results with those of competitors and other organizations delivering similar health care services.

AREAS TO ADDRESS

a. current levels and trends in key measures and/or indicators of patient satisfaction relative to competitors and/or other organizations delivering similar health care services. Results may include objective information and/or data from independent organizations, including patients. Results should be segmented by patient group, as appropriate.

b. current levels and trends in key measures and/or indicators of other stakeholder satisfaction relative to competitors and/or other organizations delivering similar health care services. Results may include objective information and/or data from independent organizations, including stakeholders. Results should be segmented by stakeholder group, as appropriate.

c. trends in gaining or losing market share to competing health care providers.

7.5 MBNQA Average Percent Score

☐ Approach ☐ Deployment ☑ Results

7.5a Does your organization collect and segment trend data that measures patient satisfaction with your services against their satisfaction with your competitors' services?

Interview notes:

MBNQA Standards

Zero-Based | World-Class

| 0 | 10 | 20 | 30 | 40 | 50 | 60 | 70 | 80 | 90 | 100 |

(Circle score that best fits your organization.)

Zero-Based Organization

- Organization collects anecdotal data on patient satisfaction relative to competitors and/or other organization delivering similar health care services.

- Organization does not collect patient satisfaction data relative to competitive organizations.

World-Class Organization

- Organization data versus comparable competitors' data show positive trends in overall patient satisfaction.

- Organization survey results, competitive awards, and ratings conducted by an independent organization show positive trends.

☐ Approach ☐ Deployment ☑ Results

Examples of Related JCAHO Compliance

The assessment process includes comparing data about the organization's processes and outcomes over time, comparing the organization's performance of processes and their outcomes to that of other organizations, including using reference databases.

7.5a   Comparative trends of patient satisfaction relative to competitors.

+ Strengths

1.

2.

3.

- Opportunities for Improvement

1.

2.

3.

Strategic Planning Issues:

    Short Term (1 to 3 years)

    1.

    2.

    Long Term (3 years or more)

    1.

    2.

220   THE BALDRIGE WORKBOOK FOR HEALTHCARE

7.5b   Does your organization collect and segment trend data that measures stakeholder satisfaction with your services against their satisfaction with your competitor's services?

Interview notes:

MBNQA Standards

Zero-Based │ 0   10   20   30   40   50   60   70   80   90   100 │ World-Class

(Circle score that best fits your organization.)

Zero-Based Organization
- *No patient/stakeholder surveys are conducted to evaluate and improve key administrative and business operations.*
- *Organization does not consistently evaluate its administrative and business operations for improved performance.*

World-Class Organization
- *Patient and stakeholder surveys are conducted within each of the administrative and business operations annually.*
- *Key process benchmarks are identified within administrative and business operations and used to gauge improvement.*

☐ Approach   ☐ Deployment   ☑ Results

Examples of Related JCAHO Compliance

The assessment process includes comparing data about the organization's processes and outcomes over time, comparing the organization's performance of processes and their outcomes to that of other organizations, including using reference databases.

7.5b   Comparative trends of stakeholder satisfaction relative to competitors.

+ Strengths

1.

2.

3.

- Opportunities for Improvement

1.

2.

3.

Strategic Planning Issues:

    Short Term (1 to 3 years)

    1.

    2.

    Long Term (3 years or more)

    1.

    2.

7.5c Do trends indicate that your organization has gained or lost market share to your competition?

Interview notes:

<pre>
                           MBNQA
   Zero-Based   Standards   World-Class
   ┌───┐
   │ 0   10   20   30   40   50   60   70   80   90   100 │
   └───┘
              (Circle score that best fits your organization.)
</pre>

Zero-Based Organization

- *Organization does not measure patient/ stakeholder turnover and relate these data to gaining or losing market share.*

- *No trend data are accumulated on patient/stakeholder loss to competing health care providers.*

World-Class Organization

- *Patient/stakeholder turnover is measured to gauge lost market share to competition.*

- *Patient/stakeholder exit interviews are conducted. Data are aggregated and used to gauge lost market share to competing health care providers.*

☐ Approach   ☐ Deployment   ☑ Results

Examples of Related JCAHO Compliance

The organization compares performance of processes and their outcomes to that of other organizations, including using reference databases.

7.5c Trends in gaining or losing market share relative to major competitors.

+ Strengths

1.

2.

3.

- Opportunities for Improvement

1.

2.

3.

Strategic Planning Issues:

    Short Term (1 to 3 years)

        1.

        2.

    Long Term (3 years or more)

        1.

        2.

Summary of Assessment Items

Transfer all assessment item percent scores from the category worksheets.

SUMMARY OF ASSESSMENT ITEMS	Total Points Possible A	Percent Score 0-100% (10% units) B	Score (A x B) C
1.0 Leadership			
1.1 Senior Executive and Health Care Staff Leadership	45	_____%	_____
1.2 Leadership System and Organization	25	_____%	_____
1.3 Public Responsibility and Citizenship	20	_____%	_____
CATEGORY TOTAL	90		_____ (Sum C)
2.0 Information and Analysis			
2.1 Management of Information and Data	20	_____%	_____
2.2 Performance Comparisons and Benchmarking	15	_____%	_____
2.3 Analysis and Use of Organizational-Level Data	40	_____%	_____
CATEGORY TOTAL	75		_____ (Sum C)
3.0 Strategic Planning			
3.1 Strategy Development	35	_____%	_____
3.2 Strategy Deployment	20	_____%	_____
CATEGORY TOTAL	55		_____ (Sum C)
4.0 Human Resource Development and Management			
4.1 Human Resource Planning and Evaluation	20	_____%	_____
4.2 Employee/Health Care Staff Work Systems	45	_____%	_____
4.3 Employee/Health Care Staff Education, Training, and Development	50	_____%	_____
4.4 Employee/Health Care Staff Well-Being and Satisfaction	25	_____%	_____
CATEGORY TOTAL	140		_____ (Sum C)

Summary of Assessment Items 225

	Total Points Possible A	Percent Score 0-100% (10% units) B	Score (A x B) C

SUMMARY OF ASSESSMENT ITEMS

5.0 Process Management
- 5.1 Design and Introduction of Patient Health Care Services ... 35 ... ____% ... ____
- 5.2 Delivery of Patient Health Care ... 35 ... ____% ... ____
- 5.3 Patient Care Support Services Design and Delivery ... 20 ... ____% ... ____
- 5.4 Community Health Services Design and Delivery ... 15 ... ____% ... ____
- 5.5 Administrative and Business Operations Management ... 20 ... ____% ... ____
- 5.6 Supplier Performance Management ... 15 ... ____% ... ____

CATEGORY TOTAL ... 140 ... ____ (Sum C)

6.0 Organizational Performance Results
- 6.1 Patient Health Care Results ... 80 ... ____% ... ____
- 6.2 Patient Care Support Services Results ... 40 ... ____% ... ____
- 6.3 Community Health Services Results ... 30 ... ____% ... ____
- 6.4 Administrative, Business, and Supplier Results ... 90 ... ____% ... ____
- 6.5 Accreditation and Assessment Results ... 10 ... ____% ... ____

CATEGORY TOTAL ... 250 ... ____ (Sum C)

7.0 Focus on and Satisfaction of Patients and Other Stakeholders
- 7.1 Patient and Health Care Market Knowledge ... 30 ... ____% ... ____
- 7.2 Patient/Stakeholder Relationship Management ... 30 ... ____% ... ____
- 7.3 Patient/Stakeholder Satisfaction Determination ... 30 ... ____% ... ____
- 7.4 Patient/Stakeholder Satisfaction Results ... 100 ... ____% ... ____
- 7.5 Patient/Stakeholder Satisfaction Comparison ... 60 ... ____% ... ____

CATEGORY TOTAL ... 250 ... ____ (Sum C)

TOTAL POINTS ... **1000** ... ____

Part III The Strategic Plan for the Health Care Organization

CHAPTER TEN

Transforming Assessment Findings into Actionable Strategies for Improvement

The assessment of the organization is complete. Now the next step is to transform the assessment results into actionable short- and long-term strategies for organizational improvement.

The assessment team should begin this process by reviewing strengths and opportunities for improvement within the areas assessed. The assessment team members will need to reach a consensus on short- and long-term strategic issues for each area. After this process is complete, the team should go back through the assessment manual and collect item percentage scores. The assessment percentages should be shaded within each appropriate item bar graph.

ORGANIZATIONAL ASSESSMENT BAR GRAPH
(Shade in assessment percentages on bar graphs from item score boxes located throughout manual.)

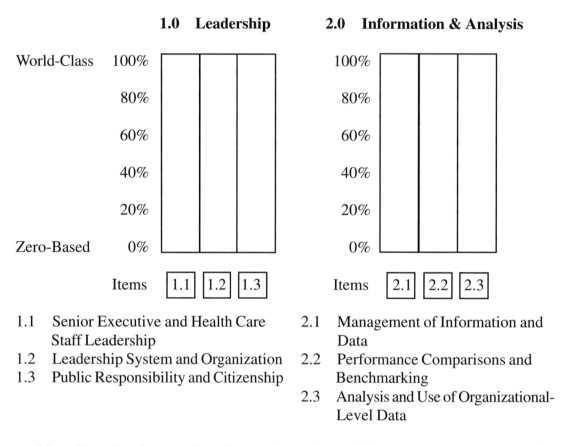

1.1 Senior Executive and Health Care Staff Leadership
1.2 Leadership System and Organization
1.3 Public Responsibility and Citizenship

2.1 Management of Information and Data
2.2 Performance Comparisons and Benchmarking
2.3 Analysis and Use of Organizational-Level Data

Note: Based on bar graphs, select and prioritize within each category short- and long-term strategic issues identified in the assessment and list below.

1.0 Leadership Category

Priority 1_____ Short term

_____ Long term

Priority 2_____ Short term

_____ Long term

Priority 3_____ Short term

_____ Long term

2.0 Information and Analysis Category

Priority 1_____ Short term

_____ Long term

Priority 2_____ Short term

_____ Long term

Priority 3_____ Short term

_____ Long term

ORGANIZATIONAL ASSESSMENT BAR GRAPH
(Shade in assessment percentages on bar graphs from
item score boxes located throughout manual.)

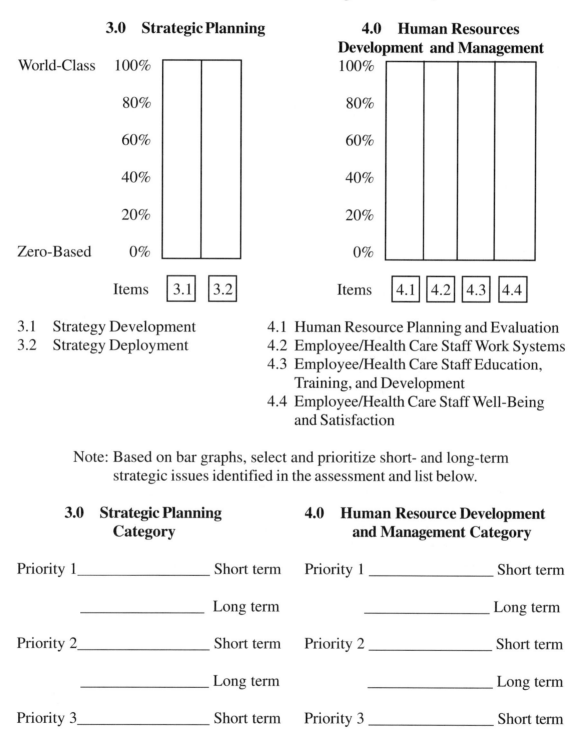

3.0 Strategic Planning

3.1 Strategy Development
3.2 Strategy Deployment

4.0 Human Resources Development and Management

4.1 Human Resource Planning and Evaluation
4.2 Employee/Health Care Staff Work Systems
4.3 Employee/Health Care Staff Education, Training, and Development
4.4 Employee/Health Care Staff Well-Being and Satisfaction

Note: Based on bar graphs, select and prioritize short- and long-term strategic issues identified in the assessment and list below.

3.0 Strategic Planning Category	4.0 Human Resource Development and Management Category
Priority 1 _____ Short term	Priority 1 _____ Short term
_____ Long term	_____ Long term
Priority 2 _____ Short term	Priority 2 _____ Short term
_____ Long term	_____ Long term
Priority 3 _____ Short term	Priority 3 _____ Short term
_____ Long term	_____ Long term

ORGANIZATIONAL ASSESSMENT BAR GRAPH
(Shade in assessment percentages on bar graphs from item score boxes located throughout manual.)

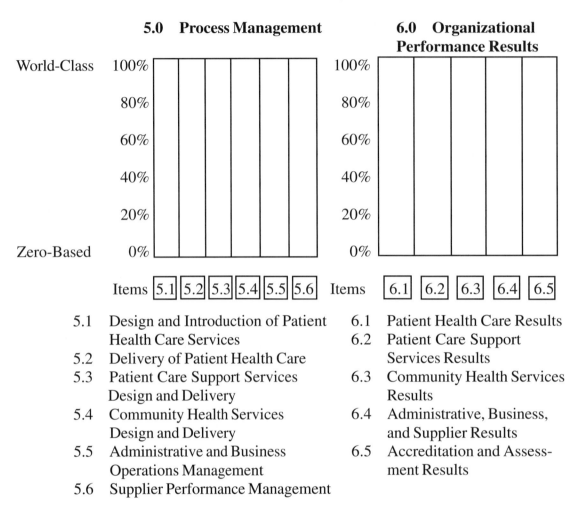

5.1 Design and Introduction of Patient Health Care Services
5.2 Delivery of Patient Health Care
5.3 Patient Care Support Services Design and Delivery
5.4 Community Health Services Design and Delivery
5.5 Administrative and Business Operations Management
5.6 Supplier Performance Management

6.1 Patient Health Care Results
6.2 Patient Care Support Services Results
6.3 Community Health Services Results
6.4 Administrative, Business, and Supplier Results
6.5 Accreditation and Assessment Results

Note: Based on bar graphs, select and prioritize short- and long-term strategic issues identified in the assessment and list below.

5.0 Process Management Category

Priority 1_____ Short term
            _____ Long term
Priority 2_____ Short term
            _____ Long term
Priority 3_____ Short term
            _____ Long term

6.0 Organizational Performance Results Category

Priority 1_____ Short term
            _____ Long term
Priority 2_____ Short term
            _____ Long term
Priority 3_____ Short term
            _____ Long term

ORGANIZATIONAL ASSESSMENT BAR GRAPH
(Shade in assessment percentages on bar graphs from item score boxes located throughout manual.)

7.0 Focus on and Satisfaction of Patients and Other Stakeholders

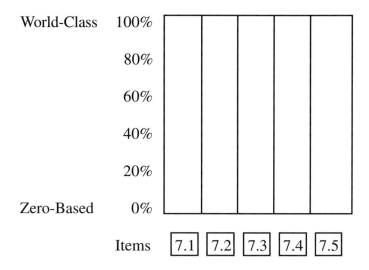

7.1 Patient and Health Care Market Knowledge
7.2 Patient/Stakeholder Relationship Management
7.3 Patient/Stakeholder Satisfaction Determination
7.4 Patient/Stakeholder Satisfaction Results
7.5 Patient/Stakeholder Satisfaction Comparison

Note: Based on bar graphs, select and prioritize short- and long-term strategic issues identified in the assessment and list below.

7.0 Focus on and Satisfaction of Patients and Other Stakeholders Category

Priority 1 _____ Short term

_____ Long term

Priority 2 _____ Short term

_____ Long term

Priority 3 _____ Short term

_____ Long term

The shaded bar graphs will help the assessment team identify specific items within each category of the organization that need improvement.

The next step for the team after all scores have been shaded in on the bar graphs is to select and prioritize short- and long-term strategic planning issues within each category that were previously identified by the team through the assessment process. The team will go through the process of prioritizing the strategic short- and long-term planning issues within each category that need to be developed into actionable improvement strategies for the organization.

After identifying and prioritizing strategic planning issues within all seven Baldrige Categories (i.e., 1.0 Leadership, 2.0 Information and Analysis, etc.), the team should reach concensus on and select the top three short- and long-term priorities offering the greatest opportunities for improvement within each category. These identified issues transform into actionable strategic initiatives (see Illustration #1).

A master strategic planning worksheet is included for the team to photocopy and use to list its prioritized short- and long-term initiatives. The appropriate category, term, and priority should be circled detailing the specific initiative. Action item(s) should be listed in respective order to accomplish the identified strategies. In addition, individual responsibilities and review and completion dates should be documented in order to transform the organization's strategic initiatives into actionable improvement. Illustration #2 details how to complete a strategic planning worksheet.

The strategic planning worksheet should be completed by the assessment overview team. The results of both the assessment and the identified strategic issues should be reported back to the organization's senior administrative leadership and ultimately integrated into the organization's annual short- and long-term strategic planning process.

ILLUSTRATION #1

1.0 Leadership

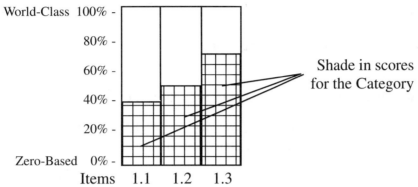

1.1 Senior Executive and Health Care Staff Leadership
1.2 Leadership System and Organization
1.3 Public Responsibility and Citizenship

Note: Based on bar graphs, select and prioritize short- and long-term strategic issues identified in the assessment and list below.

1.0 Leadership Category

Priority 1 _____ Short term
           _____ Long term

Priority 2 _____ Short term
           _____ Long term

Priority 3 _____ Short term
           _____ Long term

Top 3 Short-Term Initiatives (1 to 3 years)

Top 3 Long-Term Initiatives (3 years or more)

ILLUSTRATION #2
Strategic Planning Worksheet

Category (circle one)

- **1.0 Leadership** (circled)
- 2.0 Information and Analysis
- 3.0 Strategic Planning
- 4.0 Human Resource Development and Management
- 5.0 Process Management
- 6.0 Organizational Performance Results
- 7.0 Focus on and Satisfaction of Patients and Other Stakeholders

Term (circle one)

- **Short term: one to three years** (circled)
- Long term: more than three years

Priority (circle one) **1** 2 3   Senior Executive and Health Care Leadership to Define Quality
(List strategy here.)

ACTION ITEM(S) (Steps to accomplish strategy)	WHO IS RESPONSIBLE	REVIEW DATE	COMPLETION DATE
1. Senior staff to define quality.	President	—	January 10
2. Form two cross-functional staff teams to review definition.	Vice-President	January 30	February 28
3. Cross-functional teams to present findings to senior staff.	Team Leaders	March 2	March 30
4. Senior staff finalizes definition of quality.	President	April 5	April 30
5. Distribute definition of quality by E-mail organizationwide.	Vice-President		May 5
6.			
7.			
8.			
9.			
10.			

List action items in respective order. | List individual responsibilities by name or position. | List review dates. | List completion dates.

STRATEGIC PLANNING WORKSHEET

Category (circle one)
1.0 Leadership
2.0 Information and Analysis
3.0 Strategic Planning
4.0 Human Resource Development and Management
5.0 Process Management
6.0 Organizational Performance Results
7.0 Focus on and Satisfaction of Patients and Other Stakeholders

Term (circle one)
Short term: one to three years
Long term: more than three years

Priority (circle one) **1 2 3** _____

ACTION ITEM(S) (Steps to accomplish strategy)	WHO IS RESPONSIBLE	REVIEW DATE	COMPLETION DATE
1.			
2.			
3.			
4.			
5.			
6.			
7.			
8.			
9.			
10.			

© 1996 Donald C. Fisher and Bryan P. Simmons. The owner of this text may reproduce this worksheet for personal use only.

GLOSSARY

Health Care Organization Assessment Glossary

Accreditation - A determination by the Joint Commission that an eligible health care organization complies substantially with applicable Joint Commission standards.

Aggregated data - Data that an organization has gathered together into a mass or sum so as to constitute a whole. Aggregated data are collected and used to determine an organization's achievement levels and improvement trends.

Baldrige assessment - An organizational evaluation based on the seven categories, 28 items, and 65 areas of the Malcolm Baldrige National Quality Award Criteria for Health Care Organizations. The categories include Leadership, Information and Analysis, Strategic Planning, Human Resource Development and Management, Process Management, Organizational Performance Results, and Focus on and Satisfaction of Patients and Other Stakeholders.

Benchmarking - A method whereby teams of employees review and visit best-in-class services and practices. Benchmarking can include site visits to organizations and telephone interviews. Benchmarking is an involved process that organizations pursue when seeking to become world-class in processes that they have identified as needing improvement.

Business processes and support services - Includes units and operations involving finance and accounting, software services, marketing, public relations, information services, purchasing, and personnel.

Business ethics - A published statement of values and business ethics that are promoted and practiced both internally and externally by the organization.

Business plan - A strategic plan that is published and shared throughout the organization. Many organizations that are beginning their quality improvement process have separate business plans and quality plans.

Competitive comparisons - Comparisons of an organization's services against competitive health care organizations.

Continuous quality improvement (CQI) - A health care organization's quality improvement programs.

Control chart - A graph that is used by employees to determine if their work process is within prescribed limits.

Cross-functional teams - Teams formed from different divisions or departments to solve or create new solutions to an organizational problem or opportunity.

Cycle time - The amount of time it takes to complete a specific work process.

Data - The collection of facts, information, or statistics.

Data analysis - The study, interpretation, and breakdown of data to help the organization gauge improvement.

Documentation - The process of recording information.

Documented improvement - A process improvement that has been supported against baseline data and documented at measured intervals.

Ergonomics - The evaluation of an organization's facilities and equipment to ensure compatibility between workers and their work processes.

Employee involvement - Involvement of employees across the organization at all levels.

Employee and staff morale - The attitudes of staff in regard to their willingness to perform work tasks.

Empowerment - Employees' freedom to respond to patient and other stakeholders requests.

Flowchart - A graphic map of a work process used by employee and staff teams to document the current condition of a process.

Goals and strategies - Organizations develop goals and strategies for short-term (one to three years) and long-term (three years or more) desired results. Goals and strategies are usually written and distributed across the organization.

Health care provider - An organization that provides health care services to the public.

Health care services - All services delivered by the organization that involve professional clinical/medical judgment, including those delivered to patients and those delivered to the community.

Health care staff - Licensed providers (e.g., physicians, dentists, nurses, physician assistants, physical therapists) responsible for delivery of health care services.

Improvement plan - A written plan that the organization has published to accomplish desired improvement results.

Internal customer/supplier network - An organization's employee network, referred to as inside customers and suppliers.

Joint commission on accreditation of health care organizations - An independent, not-for-profit organization dedicated to improving the quality of care in organized health care settings. Founded in 1951, its members are the American College of Physicians, the American College of Surgeons, the American Dental Association, the American Hospital Association, and the American Medical Association. The major functions of the Joint Commission include developing organizational standards, awarding accreditation decisions, and providing education and consultation to health care organizations.

Key indicators - Key measures of performance (e.g., productivity, cycle time, cost, and other measures of effectiveness.)

Leaders, organizational - The group of individuals that set expectations, develop plans, and implement procedures to asses and improve the quality of the organization's governance, management, clinical and support functions and processes. Leaders include at least the leaders of the governing body; the chief executive officer and other senior managers; the elected and/or appointed leaders of the medical staff and the clinical departments and other medical staff members in organization administrative positions; the nursing executive and other senior nursing leaders; and other key leaders.

Management and administrative services - The activities performed to direct and conduct the affairs of a health care organization, or components thereof, as established by policies of the organization. Standards are applied to evaluate the quality of an organization's management and administrative services.

Manufacturing organization - An organization that makes or processes raw materials into a finished product.

Measurement - The process of gauging an organization's results against its customers' requirements.

Mission statement - Many organizations have a published document that defines the organization's reason for existing. The mission statement is shared with employees, suppliers, and customers.

Patient - The person receiving health care, including preventive, promotion, acute, chronic, rehabilitative, and other health care services in the continuum of care.

Patient care services - All services delivered to patients.

Patient care support services - Services that support the organization's delivery of health care services to patients (e.g., laboratory or radiology results, housekeeping services, paging services, member services, medical records and transcription services.)

Patient contact employee - An employee who directly interfaces with external patients in person, via telephone, or other means.

Patient health care services - Health care services provided directly to the patient for the purpose of prevention.

Patient relationship management - An organization's interactions and relationships with its patients and other stakeholders.

Performance data - Results of improvements in produce-and-service production and delivery processes.

Process - A series of steps linked together to provide a service for an end user.

Process control - A control device to detect and remove causes of variation in a defined process.

Process management - An organization's maintenance of defined processes to ensure that both quality and performance are continuously improved.

Productivity improvement - Measured reduction in an organization's key operational processes.

Problem-solving teams - Cross-functional, work-group, departmental, or project-focused teams that assess and analyze problems and are empowered by management to solve them.

Problem-solving tools - Tools used by teams to solve process problems (e.g., flowcharts, Pareto analysis, histograms, control charts, cause-and-effect diagrams, and matrix diagrams.)

Public responsibility - Relates to an organization's possible impact on society with its services and operations. Impact includes business ethics, environment, education, community services, and safety effects as they relate to the public.

Quality assessment - An assessment of an organization's approach to and implementation of continuous quality improvement.

Quality improvement - An approach to the continuous study and improvement of the processes of providing health care services to meet the needs of patients and others. Synonyms and near synonyms include continuous quality improvement, continuous improvement, organizationwide quality improvement, performance improvement, and total quality management.

Quality of care - The degree to which health services for individuals and populations increase the likelihood of desired health outcomes and are consistent with current professional knowledge. Dimensions of quality include the following: patient perspective issues, safety of the care environment, and the accessibility, appropriateness, continuity, effectiveness, efficacy, efficiency, and timeliness of care.

Quality plan - An organization that has just begun the quality improvement process has a written quality plan. This plan is usually separate from the business plan. Organizations that are more mature in quality usually integrate their quality plan with their business plan.

Quality results - An organization's achievement levels and improvement trends.

Quality values - The standards, beliefs, and guiding principles by which an organization operates. These values are reflected in the way employees, suppliers, and customers are treated.

Safe work practices - Organizations promote safety on the work site for employees and staff. Many health care organizations have documented guidelines for staff to follow, and they collect data on safe work practices.

Safety management - A component of a health care organization's plan, technology, and safety management program that combines five elements—general safety, safety education, emergency preparedness, hazardous materials and wastes, and safety devices and operational practices. Standards are applied to evaluate a health care organization's performance in conducting safety management programs.

Service organization - Nonmanufacturing organizations, such as utilities, schools, governments, transportation, finance, real estate, restaurants, hotels, news media, business services, professional services, repair services, and health care organizations.

Staff - All people who contribute to the delivery of the organization's services, including paid staff (employees, contractors), independent practitioners (e.g., physicians, physician assistants, nurse practitioners not paid by the organization), volunteers, and health profession students (e.g., medical, nursing, ancillary).

Stakeholders - Include family members of the patient and any individuals or groups of individuals who have a stake in services delivered by the health care organization.

Standard - A statement of expectation that defines the structures and processes that must be substantially in place in an organization to enhance the quality of care.

Standards manuals - Six Joint Commission books delineating current standards pertaining to specified types of health care organizations or services. The books are designed for use in organization self-assessment and are the basis for the survey report forms used by Joint Commission surveyors during on-site surveys.[1]

Statistical process control (SPC) - Technique for measuring and analyzing process variations.

Strategic plan - A detailed plan of action that an organization develops by establishing and defining measurable goals to achieve continuous quality improvement within an organization. A strategic plan can be broken into short-term (one to three years) and long-term (three years or more) components.

Supplier - An individual or group, either internal to the organization or external, that provides input to a work group or patient/stakeholders.

Supplier certification program - A formal supplier program that an organization uses to help improve supplier quality. Many health care organizations partner with critical suppliers and establish a relationship of trust and measurable results.

Supplier partnership - A supplier process practiced by many health care organizations. Organizations establish a preferred supplier program that is based on a trust relationship with measurable results. Supplier partnerships are usually a prelude to a more formalized supplier certification program.

Targets - Desired goals that organizations have in their strategic planning process.

Third-party survey - A patient/stakeholder or employee/staff survey conducted for the organization by a resource outside the organization.

Total quality management (TQM) - A management philosophy that focuses on continuous quality improvement (CQI) throughout the organization.

User-friendly - A process that is understandable to employees.

---

1 The six manuals published by the Joint Commission on Accreditation of Health Care Organizations are: *Accreditation Manual for Hospitals; Accreditation Manual for Ambulatory Health Care; Accreditation Manual* for *Mental Health, Chemical Dependency, and Mental Retardation/Development Disabilities Services; Accreditation Manual for Long Term Care; Accreditation Manual for Home Care;* and *Accreditation Manual for Pathology and Clinical Laboratory Services* (see p. 271 for ordering information).

Values statement - Many organizations have a published document that describes their corporate beliefs. This values statement is usually shared with staff, suppliers, and patients/stakeholders.

Vision statement - Many organizations have a published document that defies the organization's direction for the next five to ten years. The vision statement is shared with employees, suppliers, and patients/ stakeholders.

World-class organization - An organization that produces excellent results in major areas with a sound quality management approach. This organization is totally integrated with a systematic, prevention-based system that is continuously refined through evaluations and improvement cycles.

Zero-based organization - An organization that has no quality system in place. Its approach to quality management may, at best, be sound, systematic, effective, fully integrated, and implemented across the organization, but anecdotal in implementation.

APPENDIX A

Malcolm Baldrige National Quality Award for Health Care Organizations Written Application Checklist

Tips for Completing a Baldrige Award Application

This checklist will aid the assessment process by verifying the application of quality initiatives. How well and to what degree quality activities are enacted can determine how closely an organization is meeting the assessment criteria.

TIPS FOR COMPLETING A BALDRIGE AWARD APPLICATION

Many applications for the Baldrige Award are excluded early during the review process because important information is missing. Sometimes the applicant may have the missing information but did not include it. The Baldrige examiners cannot contact the applicants to clarify an application unless a site visit is planned, but only the best applications get site visits. Thus, it is imperative that the applicant complete the application as accurately and thoroughly as possible. The following are tips for those who are not experienced in completing a Baldrige application.

- Consider hiring a consultant to advise you on how to complete the application.

- Involve representatives from all major departments across the organization, both in the planning phase for the application, and in the review of application drafts. If quality is spread throughout the organization, the important information for the Baldrige application is too.

- Be sure that the vision and important goals mentioned in the leadership section are discussed appropriately throughout the application. For example, there should be strategic planning to accomplish these goals, and results of monitoring these goals should be mentioned in categories 6 and 7. Too often results are presented that have little to do with the core mission and important goals outlined earlier in the application.

- Read the application criteria carefully and provide the information that is requested. Too often the information provided is not the information that was requested. When this happens, the examiners are likely to assume that the organization did not incorporate the specific Baldrige Criteria under consideration into its operation.

This detailed checklist will aid your organization in preparing a written application for a quality award that is based on the Baldrige Criteria.

1. _____ Cite competitive benchmarking trips.
2. _____ Document and chart positive trend analyses of core processes.
3. _____ Cite examples of satisfying patients/stakeholders beyond expectations.
4. _____ Document all customer satisfaction awards received over past several years.
5. _____ Document organization's involvement with patient/stakeholder teams.
6. _____ Document outside organizations that benchmarked your organization; include letters or any correspondence received from customers.
7. _____ Retain in your files any control charts that show trends, either negative or positive, and documentation regarding what your organization did to improve negative trends.
8. _____ Insert information about your organization's corporate vision (values) statement and how it drives relationships with patients/stakeholders, employees, and suppliers.

_____ 9. Document speeches given by senior officers regarding continuous quality improvement within community/industry.

_____ 10. Document all speeches given at every employee level that refer to quality improvement within your organization.

_____ 11. Document written endorsements from major customers about the quality of your products/services, etc.

_____ 12. Solicit letters from governor or mayor acknowledging your organization's total quality initiatives.

_____ 13. Solicit letters from senior management of supplier companies who supply your organization regarding supplier partnership and certification issues.

_____ 14. Document literacy or other support program documents that help employees maintain their quality of work life.

_____ 15. Document all patient/stakeholder surveys (internal and third-party).

_____ 16. Document patient/stakeholder satisfaction letters (e.g., product and process quality).

_____ 17. Document short-term (1-3 years) and long-term (3 years or more) strategic quality plans.

_____ 18. Document your organization's integration of its quality plan into the business plan.

_____ 19. Document employee suggestion-idea system (how many employees use the system).

_____ 20. Document employee recognition (be specific when explaining how you use this to drive improvement).

_____ 21. Document quality language used in your organization's employee newsletters and videos (produce a glossary of quality terms for employees).

_____ 22. Document supplier involvement, how organization partners with suppliers and how suppliers' performance is measured.

_____ 23. Document any quality award initiatives—statewide, local, community, industry, or national—driven by the organization.

All data documented above should have a schedule to ensure completion.

Person responsible for collecting data _____.

Date assignment is due _____ Date received _____

APPENDIX B

Health Care Organizational Assessment (Based on MBNQA Criteria)

This assessment can be used to help determine to what extent a health care organization has approached and deployed continuous quality improvement (CQI) throughout its organization. A scoring analysis is provided at the end to help determine if a more thorough assessment needs to be conducted.

This quick and easy assessment can be used to measure one's own organization or to benchmark another organization's CQI program.

Leadership

	Strongly Agree 5	Agree 4	Neither Agree Nor Disagree 3	Disagree 2	Strongly Disagree 1
1. Senior executives and health care staff leadership are personally involved in quality-related activities such as goal setting, planning, reviewing company quality performance, communicating with employees and recognizing employee contributions.	❑	❑	❑	❑	❑
2. Senior executives are building quality values into the leadership process of the organization.	❑	❑	❑	❑	❑
3. Senior executives communicate quality excellence outside the organization to such groups as national, state, community, business, professional, education, health care, and government organizations.	❑	❑	❑	❑	❑
4. There is a program to communicate quality values throughout the organization.	❑	❑	❑	❑	❑
5. The organization regularly evaluates how well the quality values have been adopted throughout the organization.	❑	❑	❑	❑	❑
6. The organization involves and encourages leadership in quality at all levels of management and supervision, and each level has principal roles and responsibilities.	❑	❑	❑	❑	❑
7. The organization provides ways of promoting cooperation among managers and supervisors across different levels and different functions of the organization.	❑	❑	❑	❑	❑
8. The organization regularly reviews quality performance.	❑	❑	❑	❑	❑
9. Actions are taken to assist units not performing according to plan or goals.	❑	❑	❑	❑	❑
10. The organization evaluates the effectiveness of its approaches to integrating quality values into day-to-day management.	❑	❑	❑	❑	❑

	Strongly Agree 5	Agree 4	Neither Agree Nor Disagree 3	Disagree 2	Strongly Disagree 1
11. The organization promotes quality awareness and shares with external groups such as community, trade, business, government organizations, and other health care organizations.	❏	❏	❏	❏	❏
12. The organization has involved physician leadership in determining strategic quality goals.	❏	❏	❏	❏	❏
13. The organization encourages employee leadership and involvement in quality activities with outside organizations.	❏	❏	❏	❏	❏
14. The organization has integrated public responsibilities, such as business ethics, public health and safety, environmental protection, and waste management into its quality policies and practices.	❏	❏	❏	❏	❏

<u>Information and Analysis</u>

	Strongly Agree 5	Agree 4	Neither Agree Nor Disagree 3	Disagree 2	Strongly Disagree 1
15. Performance-based criteria are used to select quality-related data from a variety of sources, including operations and processes, employees, patients/stakeholders, suppliers, etc.	❏	❏	❏	❏	❏
16. The processes and techniques used in the organization ensure reliability, consistency, standardization, review, timely update, and rapid access to information.	❏	❏	❏	❏	❏
17. The organization regularly evaluates and improves the scope and quality of data and information.	❏	❏	❏	❏	❏
18. The organization collects competitive comparisons and benchmarks data, both inside and outside the health care industry, to support quality planning, evaluation, and improvement.	❏	❏	❏	❏	❏

	Strongly Agree 5	Agree 4	Neither Agree Nor Disagree 3	Disagree 2	Strongly Disagree 1
19. Sources of competitive and benchmark data include internal measurements, patient/stakeholder satisfaction, supplier performance, and employee information.	❏	❏	❏	❏	❏
20. The organization evaluates and improves the scope, sources, and uses of competitive benchmark data.	❏	❏	❏	❏	❏
21. The organization analyzes internal and competitive data to support its overall quality objectives.	❏	❏	❏	❏	❏
22. The organization evaluates and improves its analytical capabilities, and strives to shorten the analytical cycle and access to results.	❏	❏	❏	❏	❏

<u>Strategic Planning</u>

	Strongly Agree 5	Agree 4	Neither Agree Nor Disagree 3	Disagree 2	Strongly Disagree 1
23. The organization has established short-term and long-term plans to achieve/maintain a quality leadership position in target markets.	❏	❏	❏	❏	❏
24. The organization uses patient/stakeholder requirements, process capabilities, competitive data, and supplier abilities to develop overall business plans.	❏	❏	❏	❏	❏
25. Goal-setting and strategic-planning processes are evaluated and improved.	❏	❏	❏	❏	❏
26. The organization has established major quality goals and strategies to achieve these goals.	❏	❏	❏	❏	❏
27. The organization has short-term (1-2 year) and long-term (3-5 years) plans to commit the necessary resources to achieve key quality goals.	❏	❏	❏	❏	❏
28. Key requirements and performance indicators have been communicated to work units and suppliers.	❏	❏	❏	❏	❏
29. The organization expects significant changes in the quality levels of key product and service features over the next two to five years.	❏	❏	❏	❏	❏

Human Resource Development and Management

	Strongly Agree 5	Agree 4	Neither Agree Nor Disagree 3	Disagree 2	Strongly Disagree 1
30. The organization's human resources plans (including training, hiring, employment, and recognition) relate directly to the quality goals and strategies.	❏	❏	❏	❏	❏
31. The organization has key quality goals and improvement methods for human resource management practices such as hiring and career development.	❏	❏	❏	❏	❏
32. The organization analyzes and uses employee-related data to evaluate and improve the effectiveness of all employees.	❏	❏	❏	❏	❏
33. The organization uses specific techniques such as teams or suggestion systems to promote employee contributions and give feedback.	❏	❏	❏	❏	❏
34. The organization has increased employee authority, responsibility, and innovation.	❏	❏	❏	❏	❏
35. The organization has useful indicators to evaluate and improve employee involvement by all categories of employees.	❏	❏	❏	❏	❏
36. The organization has an effective plan to increase physician involvement in the organization's quality plan.	❏	❏	❏	❏	❏
37. The organization monitors trends and current levels of involvement by all types of employees and has established indicators of involvement for each category of employee.	❏	❏	❏	❏	❏
38. The organization has an effective system to assess what quality education and training is needed for various types of employees.	❏	❏	❏	❏	❏
39. The amount of quality education and training employees have received has increased substantially.	❏	❏	❏	❏	❏

	Strongly Agree 5	Agree 4	Neither Agree Nor Disagree 3	Disagree 2	Strongly Disagree 1
40. The organization has useful indicators to measure and improve the effectiveness of quality education and training activities.	❑	❑	❑	❑	❑
41. Employee recognition, reward, and performance measurement for individuals and groups, including managers, support the organization's quality objectives.	❑	❑	❑	❑	❑
42. Individual and group contributions to quality are recognized and rewarded.	❑	❑	❑	❑	❑
43. The organization uses key indicators to evaluate and improve its reward and performance systems.	❑	❑	❑	❑	❑
44. Employee well-being and morale factors are considered in quality improvement activities.	❑	❑	❑	❑	❑
45. Employee development is supported through mobility, flexibility, and retraining.	❑	❑	❑	❑	❑
46. Special services and facilities such as counseling, assistance, and recreational or cultural opportunities are available to employees.	❑	❑	❑	❑	❑
47. Employee satisfacton is determined, evaluated, and used in the organization's quality improvement programs.	❑	❑	❑	❑	❑
48. Trends in key indicators of employee morale, such as safety, absenteeism, attrition, satisfaction, grievances, and strikes have generally improved.	❑	❑	❑	❑	❑

Process Management

	5	4	3	2	1
49. Programs, services, and processes are developed based on patient/stakeholder needs and expectations.	❑	❑	❑	❑	❑
50. Program and service performance, as well as process and supplier capabilities, are considered when the organization reviews the designs of programs, services, and processes.	❑	❑	❑	❑	❑

	Strongly Agree 5	Agree 4	Neither Agree Nor Disagree 3	Disagree 2	Strongly Disagree 1
51. The organization evaluates and improves the effectiveness of its designs and processes and strives to shorten the design-to-introduction cycle.	❑	❑	❑	❑	❑
52. The organization assures that processes are controlled within design limits through frequent measurement of process, program, and service characteristics.	❑	❑	❑	❑	❑
53. The organization uses sound approaches to identify, correct, and verify process breakdowns.	❑	❑	❑	❑	❑
54. The organization evaluates the quality of measurements used in quality control.	❑	❑	❑	❑	❑
55. The organization uses various types of data to determine needs and opportunities for process improvements.	❑	❑	❑	❑	❑
56. The organization evaluates potential changes in processes to select the best alternative.	❑	❑	❑	❑	❑
57. The organization integrates process improvement with daily, routine process quality control.	❑	❑	❑	❑	❑
58. The organization effectively measures the quality of its systems, processes, practices, programs, and services through reviews and/or audits.	❑	❑	❑	❑	❑
59. Quality assessment findings are translated into improvements in processes, practices, training, and suppler requirements.	❑	❑	❑	❑	❑
60. The organization has an effective documentation system to track quality assurance, assessment, and improvement.	❑	❑	❑	❑	❑
61. The organization updates its documentation system to keep up with changes in technology, practice, and systems.	❑	❑	❑	❑	❑

	Strongly Agree 5	Agree 4	Neither Agree Nor Disagree 3	Disagree 2	Strongly Disagree 1
62. Quality requirement for key business processes and support services are based on internal or external stakeholder requirements and measured frequently.	❏	❏	❏	❏	❏
63. The organization has a strategy to continuously simplify and improve business processes and support services.	❏	❏	❏	❏	❏
64. The organization defines and communicates its specific quality requirements to suppliers.	❏	❏	❏	❏	❏
65. Through audits, inspections, certification and/or testing, the organization assures that its suppliers meet its quality requirements.	❏	❏	❏	❏	❏
66. The organization has an active, current strategy to improve the quality and responsiveness of suppliers through partnerships, training, incentives, recognition, and/or supplier selection.	❏	❏	❏	❏	❏

Organizational Performance Results

	Strongly Agree 5	Agree 4	Neither Agree Nor Disagree 3	Disagree 2	Strongly Disagree 1
67. The organization monitors trends in program and service quality through key measures derived from patient/stakeholder requirements and business operation analysis.	❏	❏	❏	❏	❏
68. The organization compares its current quality levels with principal competitors in the organization's key markets, industry averages, industry leaders, and world leaders.	❏	❏	❏	❏	❏
69. The organization monitors trends and current levels of key quality measures for its business processes, operations, and support services.	❏	❏	❏	❏	❏
70. The organization compares its measures of quality for business processes, operations, and support services with industry averages, industry leaders, and world leaders.	❏	❏	❏	❏	❏

	Strongly Agree 5	Agree 4	Neither Agree Nor Disagree 3	Disagree 2	Strongly Disagree 1
71. The organization measures trends and current levels of supplier quality.	☐	☐	☐	☐	☐
72. The organization compares its supplier quality with that of competitors or other appropriate benchmarks.	☐	☐	☐	☐	☐

<u>Focus on and Satisfaction of Patients and Other Stakeholders</u>

	5	4	3	2	1
73. The organization determines current and future requirements and expectations of patients and other stakeholders through objective surveys or interviews.	☐	☐	☐	☐	☐
74. The organization has a process in place to identify and prioritize the importance of product and service features to its patients/stakeholders.	☐	☐	☐	☐	☐
75. The organization evaluates and improves its processes for identifying customer requirements and expectations.	☐	☐	☐	☐	☐
76. Patients/stakeholders have easy access to the organization to comment or seek assistance.	☐	☐	☐	☐	☐
77. The organization follows up with patients/stakeholders to assess their satisfaction with products, services, or recent transactions.	☐	☐	☐	☐	☐
78. The organization's patient/stakeholder contact personnel are specially trained, empowered with decision making, recognized, and rewarded.	☐	☐	☐	☐	☐
79. The organization's technology and logistics support enables patient/stakeholder contact personnel to provide reliable and responsive service.	☐	☐	☐	☐	☐
80. The organization analyzes key patient/stakeholder-related data to evaluate costs and market consequences for policy, planning, and resource allocation.	☐	☐	☐	☐	☐

	Strongly Agree 5	Agree 4	Neither Agree Nor Disagree 3	Disagree 2	Strongly Disagree 1
81. The organization assists patient/stakeholder relationship management through such factors as accuracy, timeliness, and customer satisfaction and used this information to improve training, technology, or business practices.	❏	❏	❏	❏	❏
82. The organization has established well-defined service standards to meet patient/stakeholder requirements.	❏	❏	❏	❏	❏
83. The organization's units that support patient/stakeholder employees have standards to ensure that their support is timely and effective.	❏	❏	❏	❏	❏
84. Patient/stakeholder contact employees have a role in tracking, evaluating, and improving service standards.	❏	❏	❏	❏	❏
85. The organization makes commitments to promote patient/stakeholder trust and confidence in its services.	❏	❏	❏	❏	❏
86. Improvements in program and service quality over the past three years have been translated into stronger commitments, such as program, service, and cost guarantees.	❏	❏	❏	❏	❏
87. Formal and informal complaints made to different organizational units are compiled for evaluation and used throughout the organization, as appropriate.	❏	❏	❏	❏	❏
88. Complaints are resolved promptly and effectively.	❏	❏	❏	❏	❏
89. Complaints are analyzed to determine underlying causes and finding are translated into improvements.	❏	❏	❏	❏	❏
90. The organization evaluates and improves its complaint handling.	❏	❏	❏	❏	❏
91. The organization has an objective and valid process to determine patient/stakeholder satisfaction by segment.	❏	❏	❏	❏	❏

	Strongly Agree 5	Agree 4	Neither Agree Nor Disagree 3	Disagree 2	Strongly Disagree 1
92. The organization evaluates and improves its overall methods and measurement scales used in determining patient/stakeholder satisfaction.	❏	❏	❏	❏	❏
93. The organization monitors trends and current levels of patient/stakeholder satisfaction and segments results by groups.	❏	❏	❏	❏	❏
94. The organization monitors major indicators of adverse patient/stakeholder response.	❏	❏	❏	❏	❏
95. The organization compares its patient/stakeholder satisfaction results with key competitors and world leaders.	❏	❏	❏	❏	❏
96. The organization has received quality-related awards, recognition, or ratings from independent organizations.	❏	❏	❏	❏	❏
97. The organization has steadily gained patients and improved patient retention.	❏	❏	❏	❏	❏
98. The organization has steadily gained market share relative to major competitors.	❏	❏	❏	❏	❏
99. The organization produces documents that are user-friendly and understandable to patients and other stakeholders.	❏	❏	❏	❏	❏
100. Patient/stakeholder focus groups are used to assess new programs and services.	❏	❏	❏	❏	❏

HEALTH CARE ORGANIZATIONAL ASSESSMENT
SCORE ANALYSIS

400-500   **WORLD-CLASS**
Organization has an excellent continuous quality improvement (CQI) process in place. Organization should serve as a model for other health care providers.

200-400   **QUALITY PROGRESS**
Organization has a good CQI process in place with opportunities for improvement.

200 and Below   **ZERO-BASED**
Organization needs improvement in its CQI system. An organizationwide assessment needs to be conducted.

APPENDIX C
Benchmarking Process Checklist _____

Place a check next to each step completed.

BENCHMARKING TEAM FORMATION

_____ (1) Form a benchmarking team.

_____ (2) Identify processes within the organization that need to improve.

_____ (3) List in priority order processes that offer the greatest opportunity for improvement.

_____ (4) Select a process from the prioritized list.

_____ (5) Develop a list of organizations that are known for "best practices" regarding the identified process.

_____ (6) Reach a consensus on a maximum of three organizations to consider for a benchmark visit (Form 2).

_____ (7) Mail out, E-mail, or fax benchmarking surveys to organizations identified by the team as exhibiting "best practices" (team to use "Benchmarking Survey," Form 1).

_____ (8) Team collects benchmarking survey data (collect data on the survey Form 1).

_____ (9) Team reaches a consensus on survey scores.

_____ (10) Record survey scores onto graphs (top half of Form 2).

_____ (11) Select benchmarking site visits based on graph comparisons.

BENCHMARKING SITE VISIT

_____ (12) Team leader sends a formal letter requesting a site visit. (Note: Request no more than a three-hour visit.)

_____ (13) Send site visit questions in advance with site visit request letter. (Base questions on benchmarking survey.)

_____ (14) Request in advance any information that the host organization would like to secure from the visiting organization. (All approvals must be secured from senior leadership before the site visit is made.)

_____ (15) Select two or three team members for each site visit.

_____ (16) After all site visits have been approved, secure travel and hotel accommodations for team members at each site.

_____ (17) Collect and place all pamphlets, handouts, and data received from site visit into a benchmarking folder. All findings are to be shared back on site with the entire team.

_____ (18) Team leader sends a "thank you" letter to the host organization that was benchmarked.

BENCHMARKING SITE VISIT COMPLETED

_____ (19) Review all data collected from each site visit.

_____ (20) List key findings from each site visit ("Site Visit Benchmarking Overview", Form 3).

_____ (21) Review and reach a consensus on site visit findings.

_____ (22) Incorporate findings into process improvement ("Benchmark Process Improvement Steps," Form 4).

FORM 1: BENCHMARKING SURVEY

_____   _____
(Organization Name)   (Date of Phone Call)

Rating Scale

Do Not Know	World Class

This survey includes a series of questions to help the benchmark team determine which identified "best practices" to site visit. There are a possible 50 points that an organization can receive.

1 • 2 • 3 • 4 • 5   1. Do your consider your process to be a "best practice" within your industry?
Comments:_____
_____

1 • 2 • 3 • 4 • 5   2. Would you rate your process against competitors' organizations as being excellent, good, or fair?
Comments:_____
_____

1 • 2 • 3 • 4 • 5   3. How does your organization determine that your process is one of the "best practices" within your industry?
Comments:_____
_____

1 • 2 • 3 • 4 • 5   4. Does your organization collect process results? Will you share your results?
Comments:_____
_____

1 • 2 • 3 • 4 • 5   5. Have other organizations benchmarked your process?
Comments:_____
_____

1 • 2 • 3 • 4 • 5   6. Does your organization maintain a budget for this process?
Comments:_____
_____

1 • 2 • 3 • 4 • 5   7. How does this process contribute to increasing overall competitiveness for your organization?
Comments:_____
_____

1 • 2 • 3 • 4 • 5   8. How many employees are involved in maintaining this process?
Comments:_____
_____

1 • 2 • 3 • 4 • 5   9. How often is your process reviewed and benchmarked against other identified "best practices" inside or outside your organization?
Comments:_____
_____

1 • 2 • 3 • 4 • 5   10. What impact does this process have on overall organizational effectiveness?
Comments:_____
_____

Total Points = ☐

FORM 2: BENCHMARKING SURVEY RESULTS GRAPH

_____   _____   _____
(Organization Name)   (Organization Name)   (Organization Name)

	(Questions)		(Questions)		(Questions)
World Class	1 2 3 4 5 6 7 8 9 10	World Class	1 2 3 4 5 6 7 8 9 10	World Class	1 2 3 4 5 6 7 8 9 10
	5		5		5
	4		4		4
	3		3		3
	2		2		2
Not Done	1	Not Done	1	Not Done	1

Points _____   Points _____   Points _____

NOTE: Place a dot under each survey question number that best reflects the score from the survey (Form 1). Draw a line to connect the dots.

SITE VISIT SELECTIONS
(Based on benchmarking survey results)

Organization:_____   Team Leader:_____
Location:_____   Team Members:_____
Date:_____   _____
                                                _____

Organization:_____   Team Leader:_____
Location:_____   Team Members:_____
Date:_____   _____
                                                _____

Organization:_____   Team Leader:_____
Location:_____   Team Members:_____
Date:_____   _____
                                                _____

FORM 3: SITE VISIT BENCHMARKING OVERVIEW

Process Benchmarked:_____
Organization:_____
Location:_____
Date:_____

Key Findings:

-
-
-

Process Benchmarked:_____
Organization:_____
Location:_____
Date:_____

Key Findings:

-
-
-

Process Benchmarked:_____
Organization:_____
Location:_____
Date:_____

Key Findings:

-
-
-

FORM 4: BENCHMARKED PROCESS IMPROVEMENT STEPS

Process Benchmarked: _____

Proposed steps to be incorporated into an
improved process based on site visits.

PROCESS STEPS (Present)	PROCESS STEPS (Based on site visits)	PROCESS STEPS (Improved)
1.		
2.		
3.		
4.		
5.		
6.		
7.		
8.		
9.		
10.		

APPENDIX D
Reference List for Additional Reading

Barber, Ned. *Quality Assessment for Healthcare: A Baldrige-Based Handbook.* New York: Qualtiy Resources, 1996.

Brown, Mark Graham. *Baldrige Award Winning Quality, Fifth Edition: How to Interpret the Malcolm Baldrige Award Criteria.* New York: Quality Resources, 1995.

Fisher, Donald C., Julie E. Horine, Tricia H. Carlisle, and Stephen D. Williford. *Demystifying Baldrige.* New York: The Lincoln-Bradley Publishing Group, 1993.

Fisher, Donald C. *Measuring Up to the Baldrige.* New York: AMACOM Books, American Management Association, 1994.

Labovitz, George, Yu Sang Chang, and Victor Rosansky. *Making Quality Work.* New York: Harper Business, 1993.

Loebov, Wendy, Ed.D. and Clara Jean Ersoz, M.D. *The Health Care Manager's Guide to Continuous Quality Improvement.* Chicago: American Hospital Publishing, 1991.

Malcolm Baldrige National Quality Award 1995. *Mountainview Health System Case Study, January 1995.* Gaithersburg, MD: National Institute of Standards and Technology, 1995.

Mozena, James P. and Debby L. Anderson. *Quality Improvement Handbook for Health Care Professionals.* Milwaukee, WI: ASQC Quality Press, 1993.

Sloan, Daniel M. *How to Lower Health Care Costs by Improving Health Care Quality: Results-Based Continuous Improvement.* Milwaukee, WI: ASQC Quality Press, 1994.

APPENDIX E
Interviewing Hints and Tips

DO'S

- Be positive when asking questions.
- Allow participants time to formulate answers.
- Make sure questions are understood.
- Reword questions to aid understanding.
- Encourage all participants to answer questions.
- Appear to be interested in all respondents' answers.
- Thank participants for their time.

DONT'S

- Do not ask questions beyond what the criteria are asking.
- Never read more into the answer than is intended by the question.
- Do not ask rhetorical questions.
- Do not disagree with answers.
- Never be repetitious when asking questions.
- Do not make loaded statements when asking questions.
- Do not allow one participant to monopolize all answers.

APPENDIX F

How to Order Copies of the Baldrige Health Care Pilot Criteria and Joint Commission Accreditation Standards for Health Care Organizations

The *Baldrige Criteria* and the *Application Forms and Instructions* are two separate documents.

Individual copies of either document can be obtained free of charge from:

    Malcolm Baldrige National Quality Award
    National Institute of Standards and Technology
    Route 270 and Quince Orchard Road
    Administration Building, Room A537
    Gaithersburg, MD 20899-0001
    Telephone: 301-975-2036
    Telefax: 301-948-3716

Copies of the JCAHO 1996 Comprehensive Accreditation Manuals can be obtained by contacting:

    Joint Commission on Accredititation of Healthcare Organizations
    One Renaissance Boulevard
    Oakbrook Terrace, IL 60181-9887